the lizard way

David R. Helms

© 2019

Published in the United States by Nurturing Faith Inc., Macon GA,
www.nurturingfaith.net.

Library of Congress Cataloging-in-Publication Data is available.

ISBN 978-1-63528-086-9

Scriptures marked KJV are taken from the KING JAMES VERSION (KJV):
KING JAMES VERSION, public domain.

Cover image by UWMadison.

All rights reserved. Printed in the United States of America

This book is dedicated to my brother, Lloyd Helms, and sister, Laura Murphree. I dedicate it also to my wife, Carolyn Helms, and my son, Dave Helms, who years ago coined the phrase "the lizard way." All four of them helped me keep the lizard way open for many years.

Contents

Preface 1
When Feathers Fly 3
Taking Jesus Along 5
String Theory 7
The Power of Ten 9
Just Walk Away 12
What Would Jesus Do? Send a Puppy, of Course. 14
Laughing Gas 17
Lessons Learned 19
Alternate Universe 22
Finding Your Good Stuff 25
Two Things God Overdid 28
The Angel 30
The Lizard Way 32
Death Be Not Proud 36
Cheque, Please 39
We, the Living 42
Code Word—Mountain Dew 45
Exit 296 47
My Magic Rock 50
Caution: Horses 53
Jesus in a Bottle 55

Losing my Voice, Finding my Center 57
A Light Unto My Path 60
A Funny Story 63
The Cost of Kindness 64
ANT Problems 66
Bibliomancy: Remembering the Eagles 68
Star Stuff 71
The Gospel According to Waffle House 73
But Don't Forget Your Bucket! 76
Remembering Maggie 80
Finding Inner Joy 86
Tombstone Territory 88
Emotional Resources 91
Ordinary Wonder 94
Connections 97
Kyrie Eleison 99
4'33" 101
Acknowledgements 104

Preface

My thirteen-year-old son and I had been talking about getting a dog for some time. Finally, during mid-December of 1994, we went to the Chattanooga Humane Society to get a dog. My son had said for weeks, "I don't want no girl dog." He was capable of better grammar, but that's what he said (later he graduated from Georgia Tech and Purdue University). The gentleman who showed us through the kennel led us to a cage where all we saw was a lump of black fur. He picked up one of the dogs to reveal that there were two dogs in that pile of fur, a male and a female. Was it her eyes, one blue and brown, and the other sky blue? Or was it those beautiful brown and white markings on her jet-black body? I don't know, but it was the "girl dog" that we left with. We paid our $25, signed some papers stating that we would take good care of her, and took Maggie home. After we bathed her (twice) we laid her on my bed for her to take a nap. Over the next weeks and months, she grew into the most beautiful mixed shepherd that you can imagine. And her quiet and gentle disposition was noticed by friends and strangers for years to come. You can read all about that in my essay, "Remembering Maggie."

In 2007, Maggie developed a brain tumor behind her right eye. After giving her the best year possible, the day came to have her put to sleep. On March 13, 2008, after the veterinarian performed that awful task, I stayed with Maggie a few minutes, then left. The veterinarian's office took care of her remains. What follows are stories, "essays" that Maggie inspired in me. It is my highest hope that in reading my experiences and my innermost thoughts and feelings, you will not only enjoy my journey, but also find meaning for yourself. You can read my essay, "4'33''" for more on that. The book I wrote and the book you read are entirely different books. Each story represents some experience, some memory, some idea, some feeling that is uniquely mine, but these words will trigger totally different memories, ideas, and feelings in you. Maybe you will be inspired to write your thoughts and feelings, too. No one can write your stories but you. In a few years, I look forward to reading each one. "The Lizard Way" is one of my stories that you will find here. It is perhaps the most significant. I think that you may discover that you have many lizard ways of your own.

So get a cup of coffee, a glass of tea, a glass of wine, or whatever helps you to relax. Settle down in a comfortable chair and enjoy my journey. I know writing these stories has been one of the best parts of my pilgrimage. To quote a friend of mine who says this often as he starts his truck, "Here we go."

When Feathers Fly

And I thought "feathers flying" was just a figure of speech. After the squirrels destroyed my bird feeder, I hung a finch sock and let it go at that. I have enjoyed seeing the little birds come and go and seeing the vast varieties of colors on these marvelous creatures.

Yesterday morning, I was enjoying a cup of coffee and watching two of the yellow finches share the sock. Well, share would not be the proper word. To my amazement, they got into it and yellow feathers flew everywhere! It was quite a spectacle to see these usually docile little birds get at each other like that. It was apparent to me that if one had simply waited about five seconds, the sock would have been vacant, and the altercation would have been unnecessary.

So are we to wonder about the "human" nature of these little creatures? Are they much different from the way we fly off the handle and get at each other's throats over little or nothing? Recently, I watched a traffic altercation in New York City between a driver and a pedestrian. Although the pedestrian had the right of way, the driver turned in front of the woman and cut her off. She slapped the hood of his car and loudly yelled at the driver, while saluting him with her right hand, or a part thereof. It was not a close call where life and limb were concerned, but it was a close call to her.

On an international scale, war was barely averted in 1859 when an American resident of the San Juan Islands shot and killed a pig belonging to a British resident. Tempers were already short because of an ongoing dispute over the property rights of the United States and British North America. Warships were dispatched and seamen on both sides readied themselves for war. Amazingly, and rare in the history of military confrontation, no shots were fired. The war that didn't happen is still called The Pig War to this day. Thankfully, the pig was the only casualty.[1]

Maybe flying feathers are inevitable, but it seems to me that we could all choose our battles more carefully. Whether it's walking across a busy street in New York City or getting upset over a dead pig, you would think we could learn to count to 10 before shooting birds or dispatching warships. Also, when we ruffle feathers, we can apologize if we need to, and strive to make relationships better instead of worse. As for that pig in the San Juan Islands, I'm sure it became someone's breakfast within a few days. Pigs tend to die young anyway.

[1] https://en.wikipedia.org/wiki/Pig_War_(1859)

Taking Jesus Along

I saw a church sign yesterday that really set me off. The admonition on the sign was: DON'T FORGET TO TAKE JESUS ALONG ON YOUR VACATION. The fact is that most church signs annoy me, and this one was no exception. However, instead of staying annoyed, I decided to put the sign to good use. I let it inspire mental gymnastics for my own entertainment and enlightenment. I decided to try and figure out what the author of that sign had in mind! In this particular case, a Baptist church housed the sign. While it really doesn't matter which denomination posts annoying signs, I grew up in a Southern Baptist church, so I decided that perhaps there was significance.

For starters, many South Alabama Baptists are agin' more than they are for. They are agin' drinking, dancing, short skirts, gambling, homosexuality, heterosexuality, movies, Panama City, and a plethora of other sins. In my childhood and young adult days, preachers warned us of the dangers of "mixed bathing," which has nothing at all to do with bathing, but simply warns that boys and girls should not swim together. Heaven only knows what that could lead to!

When I was growing up, my father, a Southern Baptist deacon, let us play cards, even poker, but we weren't allowed to wager anything—not pennies, matchsticks, toothpicks, or any other item. As we got older, "drinking" was of course forbidden—no amount of alcohol was to be tolerated at all. And while smoking was discouraged, since our home and car were filled with cigarette smoke, not much was said about it.

So, with these things in mind, what could that church sign mean? In the first place, how the heck do you "take Jesus along" with you on vacation? Don't Christians believe that Jesus is always in their hearts? Don't we preach the passage from Psalm 139:7 where the psalmist says that you can never escape God's presence? Take Jesus along? Does this mean that if you go to Panama City on vacation that your teenaged daughter should wear a one-piece swimsuit with a frilly bottom? Take Jesus along? "Do not drink any alcoholic beverage, not even the fruity drinks with umbrellas in them" while having dinner at Captain Anderson's? WWJD? Forget the fact that Jesus' first miracle was to miraculously change several hundred gallons of water into several hundred gallons of fine wine for people who reportedly had already had a bit too much to drink. That was then. This is now.

"Take Jesus along." Maybe that means to take your Bible with you on vacation. That's not a bad idea. Reading the Acts of the Apostles while on the beach and listening to the surf gives the activities around the Sea of Galilee a whole new perspective. And "taking Jesus along" probably means to take some dress clothes and find a church to visit on Sunday morning. After all, "taking Jesus along" on vacation is a kissing cousin to "don't take a vacation from God."

One of my favorite stories in the Bible is recorded in Luke, Chapter 24. This passage tells the story of two men walking on the road to Emmaus toward Jerusalem. In this familiar story, as the men are walking, they are discussing the events of the previous days, and as they walk, Jesus himself walks up and joins the conversation. He asks them whom they are discussing, and they are bewildered that there could be anyone who wouldn't know about what happened to Jesus of Nazareth! Jesus ends up eating with them in their village, and when he broke bread, they recognized him. They didn't go looking for Jesus; he had been looking for them. It's hard to go on vacation without taking Jesus along—he has a way of staying close by. And you don't even have to hide the wine.

String Theory

Sibling: One of two or more individuals having one common parent

    Our piano tuner was here earlier this week. It's expensive, but necessary, maintenance if you want to keep your piano in good shape. Getting my piano tuned will not only make the piano much more pleasant to play and to hear, but will extend the life of the instrument as well. If you don't get the piano tuned from time to time, it will eventually be unable to hold a tune. The wooden bridge that holds the pegs tight gets used to being slightly out of adjustment and will prefer to stay that way indefinitely.

    Last Friday, I had lunch with my brother and sister. We met in a restaurant in Panama City, Florida, and we laughed and talked for almost two hours. I have spent time with each of them several times over the years, but it seldom works out that the three of us are in the same place at the same time. During our lunch, we talked about a lot of things. We reminisced about our lives and childhood, as conversation bounced around 102 Glenn Street, Enterprise, Alabama, where we shared our formative years with our mother, father, and several cats and dogs. It was good to connect with both of them and remember the time we shared together on Glenn Street, and the relationships that, for better or worse, have shaped our lives. In spite of it all, the three of us still resonate. We didn't discuss our little brother who only lived eight days, but we realize that he made his silent yet profound statement about our family line as well. His life resonates as loudly as any of the three of us. We would from time to time break our mother's spirit—he broke our mother's heart.

    There are a little more than 200 strings on a piano and none of them are the same. They are similar in length and temperament, but each of them is slightly different. Not even the two or three strings of the same note are exactly the same. It's the things that are the same that make it a nice piece of furniture, but it's the intricate differences that make the piano an instrument of music.

The DNA of my older brother, my younger sister, and my DNA are entirely different. Although we at different times shared the same womb, our chromosomes from the same two people swirled into being in dramatically different ways. In spite of that, our human bond is unique in the entire world. I hold in reverence the things that make us the same, but I celebrate as well the things that make us different.

The string theory, which has its roots in Einstein's General Theory of Relativity, is a scientific theory that unites everything in the universe. "It is also called TOE, the Theory of Everything, a unification of all known fundamental forces in the cosmos and within ourselves" (Wikipedia). I'm fairly sure that our lunch conversation didn't solve any of the riddles of the universe, but it did remind me of one significant thing. The strings that bind our hearts are inextricably woven into the fabric of everything. I don't love my brother and sister more than I love the rest of my immediate family—I just loved them first.

I don't play our piano that often, or all that well, but when I walk by it I get a lot of pleasure just knowing that it's in tune again. Tune-ups are necessary for extending the life of anything.

The Power of Ten

Museum: building, place, or institution devoted to the acquisition, conservation, study, exhibition, and educational interpretation of objects having scientific, historical, or artistic value

I was born to please. It is my pleasure to please. If you're happy, I'm happy. I hope it makes you happy for me to say that.

Recently, I bought a travel guide for New York City. It didn't take me long to find the section on art galleries and museums. I never tire of viewing international art, space museums, and American natural history. It always boggles my mind that I am actually looking at the real deal and not a copy or replica. It's not only the original; it's the one and only.

As I was looking through my guide, my thoughts trailed back to a business trip to Washington, D.C., many years ago. I was a financial advisor with IDS Financial Services, and we sold a variety of financial services and products to our clients. For whatever reason, I was often fascinated by those offbeat investments that other reps didn't get excited about. One of those was a real estate investment trust offered by Shurgard, a company based in Seattle, Washington. The investment packaged high quality mini-storage warehouses all over the United States. The investor received pass-through income from rented units. At this particular time, Shurgard was hosting a meeting in Washington, D.C., and, since I was the only rep in our office who had actually looked at their prospectus, I was asked to attend the meeting. An all-expense paid trip to the nation's capital seemed like a good idea to me, so I accepted the invitation. The meetings were held on Thursday and Friday morning, and were informative and productive, as I later became a division leader in sales of the Shurgard product. The meetings concluded early Friday afternoon, and as my flight home wasn't scheduled until Saturday afternoon, I had all of Friday afternoon and evening, as well as Saturday morning to explore D.C.

Now, when you're born to please, this is not as pleasurable as you would think! I had never before been given so much discretionary time and money to explore such a large place in all my life. There was a vast array of decisions before me, and nobody to defer to! It was just me—and me.

Friday afternoon, after careful consideration, "we" ventured to the National Gallery of Art. To say the least, I was amazed and deeply affected by the beauty of what I saw there. The art of Picasso, Monet, Renoir, Degas, and scores of other world-renowned artists were on display, and it was just too much to take in. Later in the afternoon, I had to decide where to eat. When I walked past one particular jazz bar and there was no line to enter, I was tempted, but opted for a nice, quiet restaurant. During dinner, I read about the bar I had walked past and found it to be rated as the best jazz bar in the city, if not the country. To correct the error of my ways, I decided to visit it after dinner, but by then there was a long line out the door and down the street, so I walked on. The next morning, "we" decided to go to the Smithsonian's Air and Space Museum. By now the pressure was getting to me—I needed someone to talk to and weigh in on all the decision-making. The problem didn't get better when I got to the museum! Do you know how BIG the Air and Space Museum is? Do you know the number of exhibits available? I was absolutely wearing myself out considering myself. I considered approaching a perfect stranger to ask his opinion. Okay, not really.

Of all the exhibits that I enjoyed there, of all the spectacular one-of-a-kind things that were displayed, from the Wright brothers' plane to the Spirit of St. Louis, to the Mercury capsule, and the Apollo spacesuits, the exhibit that I most remember was The Power of Ten. This display was in a very small cubbyhole, off to the side of the flow of traffic, so that I almost missed it. I walked over and what I saw blew my mind. There before me was a computer generated display that graphically demonstrated the awesome power of ten, from the far reaches of the universe to the smallest quantum particles inside our skin. And with the power of ten, it only took a few keystrokes at their terminal, one multiple of 10 at a time, to go from one end of the universe to the other. Exponential, to say the least. It was the most profound math and science I had ever experienced. That's what happens in a museum sometimes—you become something you have never been before. The gray matter rearranges itself in a completely new way. That's why all the stuff in museums is there. We all need to see it from time to time.

I think such a trip taken alone wouldn't be nearly as difficult now that I'm older and wiser, but, thankfully, when I go to New York soon there will be four other people with me to share in the responsibility of making the decisions of where to go and what to see. The power of five may not be as dramatic as the power of ten, but it beats the heck out of the power of one.

Just Walk Away...

A good friend of mine suggested that I watch the movie *The Search for Christopher Robin*. So I did. At first, I was put off by the talking stuffed animals. But as the movie progressed, they became less like stuffed animals and more like living, breathing creatures. As I listened to their dialogue, I was deeply affected by their opinions and philosophies of life. Pooh tells Christopher Robin several times that he is a "bear of small brain," but he had plenty enough brain to offer rich concepts of abundant living.

I didn't write down or memorize these statements or these truths. If I watch the movie again, I'll stop and write down some of the quotes. Pooh said something though that has stayed with me: "When I want to get somewhere, I walk away from where I've been."[1]

If you're in a soul-numbing, dead end job, just walk away.
If you're addicted to narcotics or alcohol, just walk away.
If you're in a destructive relationship, just walk away.
If you're prone to worry and anxiety, just walk away.
If you're hanging on to anger and resentment, just walk away.
If you're hanging on to guilt and remorse, just walk away.
(add your troubling issue), just walk away.

"Walking away" also involves "walking toward." You may need to stay in your job until you find a new one or are financially able to move on. You may need more education to become qualified for that dream job. You may need to walk toward a counselor who can provide therapy and help. You may need to walk toward a psychiatrist who can prescribe medicine and counsel to guide you through withdrawal and chemical dependence. You may need to find a shelter for battered women to provide temporary protection and relief from physical and emotional harm. You may need to confide in and lean on a friend who can offer love and support as you find your way. You may need to find a church, where caring people can help ground you in eternal truths. You may need to walk away from a church that offers easy answers for every problem. Finally, like Pooh, you may need to reach inside yourself to rediscover your center and become reacquainted with yourself, your priorities, principles, and hopes and dreams.

In one dramatic scene, Christopher Robin woke up, realized that he had overslept and said, "Oh no! It's tomorrow!" to which Pooh replied, "It's usually today." And if a journey of 1,000 miles begins with a single step, today is as good a day as any to take it. Now you have to figure out which way to go. Pooh used Christopher Robin's compass to go north. If you're not quite sure which direction to go, north is as good as any. Better yet, take inventory of your options and choose the one that you think is best. Pooh asked, "What day is it, Christopher Robin?" "It's today," he replied. To which Pooh said, "Ah, today. My favorite day."[2]

[1] *Pooh's Grand Adventure: The Search for Christopher Robin*, DVD, (Burbank, CA: Buena Vista Home Entertainment, 2006).

[2] *Pooh's Grand Adventure: The Search for Christopher Robin*.

What Would Jesus Do? Send a Puppy, of Course…

In 1896, Charles Sheldon's book, *In His Steps*, was published. The book has sold over 30 million copies worldwide. The full title of this novel is *In His Steps: What Would Jesus Do?* Besides becoming a mantra for Christians everywhere, WWJD has become a marketing phenomenon including jewelry, clothing, and a variety of other things. There should be warning labels on the merchandise that you could be playing with fire. Most people who wear this jewelry have little idea what it means.

I became a Christian at the ripe old age of 10. You could argue that a 10-year-old boy in a Southern Baptist home in the buckle of the Bible belt had little need for salvation. But between hearing evangelist R.G. Lee preach his famous "Pay Day Someday" sermon and my own internal fear of hell, I wasn't going to take any chances. I got saved!

Seven years later, our youth director challenged our youth group to "sell out to God"—to give ourselves completely to Jesus Christ. At first glance, this sounds like a good thing, and he certainly meant it that way. On the surface, it looked like a commitment that would transform my life and transform the lives around me. The decision to "sell out" did transform my life, but not in the way it was intended. With that directive, my youth director handed me a keg of powder. When he put a copy of *In His Steps* in my hand, he lit the fuse.

Before every decision I made, I asked myself, "What would Jesus do?" and then I tried to do exactly that. E-x-a-c-t-l-y that. What I figured out very quickly was that it is very difficult to know what Jesus would do in every situation. For that matter, it was hard to decide what Jesus would do in most situations. But that didn't stop me from trying. What my youth director failed to tell me is that only Jesus knows what Jesus would do. The attempt of WWJD would become an exercise in futility, total frustration, and self-destruction. Within about six months, my mother sought him out and said, "You have ruined my son. I want the old David back." He assured her that my commitment was genuine and that she had nothing to worry about. He was wrong.

Instead of becoming more like Jesus, I became more like the Pharisees who hated him. Those devout religious leaders dogged him, tormented him and eventually sent him to the cross, all in the name of God. I was gradually becoming more rigid, dogmatic, judgmental, and unloving in every way possible. I alienated my family, my closest friends, my classmates, and even my teachers. And besides all of that, I was miserable. I was absolutely miserable. There is medicine for depression, anxiety, and many other emotional ills, but there is nothing you can take for misery. To bite off this kind of rigid commitment to what I thought Jesus would do was to create a black hole. All light went in, but no light came out. I was descending into the hell that I feared as a child.

It took a bizarre string of events over a period of time to help me out of this quagmire I had created for myself. And through these events, I began to experience some relief. What started as a trickle of positive emotion became a wellspring of love, joy, and authentic relationships. Several things happened including a divine appointment with a bowl of turnip greens that my mother prepared (think "and God prepared a worm"). But perhaps the most significant thing happened in front of my friend Danny's house. He was disabled and couldn't drive, so I drove him to many of our functions. We had been to a youth prayer meeting at church. Sitting in the car, I thought, "What would Jesus do?" He would pray some more, so that's what we did. While Danny was praying, I kept my eyes open. I noted a small puppy in his yard. To my utter amazement, the little puppy walked up under a child's football helmet and got the helmet on his head. The right way! The puppy started running around the yard with the football helmet on his head in gleeful abandon. I started laughing uncontrollably. Danny thought I got the Holy Ghost and started shouting praises to God! I said, "No, look!" and he started laughing too. It felt good to laugh. I had not laughed in months.

I would like to tell you that I was cured of my spiritual cancer on the spot, but it would take much longer for that to happen. But what that puppy did had begun a process of healing, as I thought, "Here I am the crown of creation and that little dog is having a better time of it than I am. God created me for abundance and joy."

What I have learned from all of this is that Jesus never asked me to try to live like him; he only asks me to allow him to live through me. I'll never walk on water. I'll never feed a multitude with a few loaves and fishes. I'll never heal a blind man. He never asked me to. I read recently in *Baptists Today*, "It's not important to ask yourself, 'What would Jesus do?' The question you need to ask yourself is: 'What did Jesus do?'" So, Mr. Sheldon, you may have sold 30 million copies, but you missed the point, and I missed the point. WDJD? He always did the loving thing. In each and every situation he found himself in, he loved the other person unconditionally. He loved the fishermen, the tax collectors, the prostitutes, the Pharisees, the Samaritans, the woman at the well, and his best friends Mary, Martha, and Lazarus. In the movie, *Resurrection*, there was a sign in the window of an old southwestern filling station that read, "God is love and vice versa." So do the loving thing and you've done the *Jesus* thing. If you just do this, you won't have to remember either acronym; they will take care of themselves.

Laughing Gas

Nitrous Oxide: commonly known as happy gas or laughing gas; chemical compound with the chemical formula N2O

On one particular visit to the dentist, in addition to Novocain, my dentist offered nitrous oxide as well. I had never had an occasion to be given nitrous oxide, since I typically did just fine without it, but I was having a wisdom tooth extracted. The dentist explained to me that the root of the tooth was embedded beneath another tooth and this would be a difficult extraction, so I might want to consider the additional medication.

One never looks forward to these procedures, but as the day came around, I wasn't concerned about it at all. I took my place in the chair; the hygienist placed the cannula in my nose and explained to me that if I felt I was going "under too far," I should just breathe through my mouth. Sounded simple enough! As this magic chemical started to get into my system and take effect, I became more and more relaxed, and soon felt that I didn't have a care in the world. I was indeed doing fine. As the experience continued, I started sinking down through the chair to the floor. I felt as if my body was drifting down, down, down. At some point, I decided that I didn't like the way it felt, so I started trying to breathe through my mouth as he had instructed. The only problem was that I kept sinking lower and lower, going down, down. It occurred to me that perhaps my mouth wasn't really open, so with what little motor control I had left, I raised my hand to my lips, only to find that indeed my mouth was closed. I pulled the corner of my mouth open with my index finger, and immediately felt the rush of oxygen to my brain. Very quickly, my head began to clear and my body floated back up into my chair.

I sat there for several more minutes and thought, "The whole idea is to be relaxed and avoid pain!" So I closed my mouth and again allowed myself to fall under the influence of the gas. This time, my thoughts took a different route. I found myself thinking, "Laughing gas. I wonder why they call this stuff laughing gas?" As quickly as the thought came to me, I began to chuckle. "Laughing gas! What a strange thing to call this." And I chuckled again. Then I started to laugh out loud, and once it started, I simply couldn't stop. "Laughing gas!!" I was laughing so hard my sides were beginning to hurt. I couldn't remember a time ever laughing to hard. I could see the headlines: "Rossville Man Dies Laughing in Dentist's Chair." When the hygienist came in to check on me, I was relieved. She, too, began to laugh, and I realized that four other people were standing in the doorway laughing with us. I was dying! I began to envision other headlines: "Rossville Man Sues Dentist for Allowing Rib Fractures Due to Laughing." Finally, my caregiver reached over and made an adjustment, and I was able to get control of myself. A long hour or two later, the dentist had used everything except a jackhammer to extract my tooth and complete the procedure.

While not everyone who is crying is sad, it's good to remember that not everyone who is laughing is happy!

Lessons Learned

In 1992, I owned a 1987 Honda Accord, a five speed on the floor. I loved that car—everything about it! Its sleek body style and hideaway headlights gave me the feeling of driving a sports car. For me, it was a sports car—a poor man's Porsche.

At that time, I worked with a great bunch of guys at IDS/American Express, and the same group of guys went to lunch together every day. Around 11:45 a.m. or so, someone would start the "What's for lunch?" conversation, and on this particular day, I offered to drive us around the corner, and we all piled into my Honda.

The parking lot sat beside a service station, which sat below the restaurant, and the lot ended at a wall separating the two businesses. The thing you need to understand in order to appreciate the drama about to unfold is this: from the perspective of the service station, there was a 10-foot wall, but from the perspective of the parking lot of the restaurant, the "wall" was only about six inches high with a drop off of about 10 feet to the asphalt parking lot of the station. So…

We got out of the car, I locked it, and we began walking toward the restaurant. Have you ever just out of the blue gotten a bad feeling? Well I had gotten a bad feeling about my car and turned around to see it rolling slowly backwards toward the "wall" beneath it. It's possible, of course, that I heard it, but I think I just felt it. Apparently, I had left the car in neutral and failed to engage the parking brake. I had about 20 seconds to stop the car and it took me about two of those seconds to decide what to do. Stop the car!! This was well before the days of remote entry. It was just my car keys, my split-second reflexes, and me. It never occurred to me at the time that I should not put myself in harm's way and should have let the car roll to certain death. I was only thinking of saving my Accord, so I jumped into action, knowing that everything could only be done once. As I ran toward the car, I was reaching for my keys, and retrieved them from my pocket while jogging beside the rolling vehicle. While trotting alongside the car, I found the key on the ring and attempted to insert the key into the door while the car gained speed. Pay dirt! The key went in. I turned it, unlocked the door, opened the door, and with seconds left before catastrophe, I managed to get into the car and apply the brake. Only then did "What kind of fool am I?" begin playing in my head. I just sat there for a minute to get my wits about me. Now the second problem became clear to me—straight shift cars, as you know, will roll backwards a few feet when you move your foot from brake to gas pedal and engage the clutch, and I didn't have a few feet to spare! Thankfully, I had perfected the art of using the handbrake during those sensitive maneuvers and trusted my skills not to fail me. I started the car, put it in first gear, and pulled up the hand brake. In the same motion, I released the clutch, moved my foot from brake to gas pedal, and engaged the accelerator as I released the hand brake. The car moved forward as I had hoped and prayed. I had saved my car. My friends were kind enough to wait a few minutes before they died laughing. About two minutes, as I recall.

Lessons learned:
1. You can't always trust your feelings, but most of the time they're trying to tell you something.
2. Don't leave your car in neutral without the brake on.
3. If your car starts rolling and you aren't in it, it's better to call Geico than 911 (even a cave man knows that!).
4. Things are just things. Don't risk life and limb for things. Risk life and limb for flesh and blood, but not for things.

This story could have ended in several different ways. I could have never turned around and I would have heard my car crash to the pavement. I could have run along beside the car and failed to get the door open and watched in horror as my "sports car" crashed to the pavement. I could have opened the door, gotten into the car, and crashed to the pavement along with my car. Air bags won't do a lot of good when you're going backwards. But all's well that ends well. Well, almost. About six months later, I blew the engine in my little Honda and had to give it a decent burial after all. Another good thing about that day is that my friends picked up lunch in gratitude that they didn't have to walk back to the office.

Alternate Universe

In 1982, I was the minister of music and youth at a church about five miles from where I now sit. Since we left that position and that church, our lives have gone in multiple directions, but we never left the Rossville/Ringgold/Fort Oglethorpe area of Georgia. There were so many things that I loved about that church and that job, but I particularly enjoyed my relationships with those young people and our incredible youth choir. Choir tours. Youth retreats. Lock-ins. Cookouts. Youth rap. But other areas of the job were going south, and I need to leave. I was contacted by a church in Atlanta, Georgia, to talk about the prospect of joining their staff in the same position, minister of music and youth. All conversations were going well, with nothing but green lights and blue skies between that position and me. In my mind, I was headed to a large suburban Atlanta church with many opportunities for ministry and personal growth. It seemed to be a perfect fit for me, and they were as excited as I was. During the weeks that I was interviewing with this church, I attended a conference in Nashville, Tennessee, and was introduced to a philosophy of youth ministry that they called The Four Phases of Ease. During my last interview with the Atlanta youth committee, I talked about this philosophy and how interested I was in its concepts. The interview went well—or so I thought—but several days went by and I hadn't heard anything from anyone in Atlanta. After several days, a staff member called and informed me that they had decided to go in a different direction. He told me, "The comments you shared made the committee think that you were going to major on the music ministry and minor on the youth, if not ignore them altogether." Nothing could have been further from my intent, and I was shocked. I questioned myself over and over—why didn't I just share with them my love for young people and youth ministry? Why didn't I just tell them how much I enjoyed ministering to young people? I was devastated! Youth ministry and youth music were my passions. I kicked myself to kingdom come.

Within a year, as things continued to deteriorate, I became totally frustrated and discouraged, and resigned my position with no job and nowhere to go. Typically, when ministers do that, they avail themselves of limited options—sell cars, life insurance, or real estate. I chose the latter, and after three years of moderate success, became a financial advisor with IDS/American Express, a position I would hold for the next 12 years.

For two years at IDS, we were given warning: things were changing, and unless we wanted to take a comprehensive exam, we were encouraged to enroll in CFP promptly. I ignored the warning and didn't enroll. I felt that I just wasn't mentally or financially prepared to begin the rigorous process of studying for the Certified Financial Planner exams. By the time I got involved, the comprehensive final was a requirement. But I thought, "If I've passed all the exams, then passing a final shouldn't be a problem." I was wrong. Over the next three years, I studied and passed the most grueling six exams I had ever tackled. I had thought the Series 7 exam was the hardest one I would ever take. Again, I was wrong. For each exam I put in countless hours of study. I studied at home, in the library, in restaurants; anywhere I could find a table and a chair. After failing two of the exams, income tax and estate planning, I took live courses and passed both. For those three years, I ate and slept CFP tests. I was committed to the designation—it mattered to me.

When I started studying for the comprehensive exam, I realized that I had made a serious mistake in putting off my enrollment. The material was different and involved complicated case studies for families and businesses—budget planning, education planning, retirement and insurance planning, and more. With only a business calculator, I was required to make exact calculations that would span 20 or 30 years in all of these areas. The exam was a multiple-choice test, so every question had to be exactly to the dollar. Right or wrong. As a final assault on the task ahead, I took a two-week cram course, and for eight hours a day for 10 days, we drilled on passing the CFP exam. The irony of the fact that I was sitting in Atlanta for this brutal session didn't go unnoticed.

Test day finally came. It was a 10-hour exam, four hours on Friday and six on Saturday. As I left the testing center, I knew two things: one, that I had failed the test and two, I wouldn't take it again. Within a year, I resigned my position as a financial advisor and moved on.

Sometimes I can't help but wonder where other roads might have led. It's logical to assume that I wouldn't be writing about CFP exams had I gone to the church in Atlanta. It's also logical to assume that, had I passed that final exam, I would still be in the finance world somewhere. Those two outcomes, however, are mutually exclusive and I'll never know.

Although I have enjoyed three totally different career paths, we still live within five miles of where we landed in 1979. And, although Robert Frost suggested that the road not taken could never be traveled, what if in some sense it can?[1] What if somehow and somewhere, a part of me took that job in Atlanta and my life went off in that direction? What if, somehow, further down that second road, I passed that exam with flying colors and I'm still meeting with clients helping them to plan their futures and handing them my CFP business card? What if there really are wormholes that open up to alternate universes where we start again and do things differently, do things better? If heaven is forever, we're going to be doing something all the time, aren't we? You can only sing "Amazing Grace" for so long, after all.

Meanwhile, I wouldn't trade the life I have for anything in the world. I don't want to be anywhere this morning other than where I sit, scratching up these words to you and me. If I, in fact, only get to travel one of these paths, I'll choose this road hands down, the road that I now travel. And, as Frost concludes, "That has made all the difference."[2]

[1] Robert Frost, "The Road Not Taken," in *Robert Frost's Poems*, ed. Louis Untermeyer (New York: Henry Holt and Company, 1971), 219.

[2] "The Road Not Taken"

Finding Your Good Stuff

Joseph Campbell, the famous professor of comparative mythology, was most well known in academic circles until Bill Moyers made him famous to the world. Campbell died in 1987, and a year later PBS aired a six-part documentary called *The Power of Myth*. In this series, Moyers interviewed Campbell about his life, his loves, and his core beliefs.[1] They delved into myths from around the world, and how they guide our lives if we let them. This documentary was then published as a coffee table book, *The Power of Myth* and it subsequently adorned the living rooms of thousands of homes around the world. Who reads a coffee table book anyway? Well, I did. I then went on to read several of his published books, five of them being *The Masks of God* series and *The Hero with a Thousand Faces*. I became supersaturated in his notion that myth is inherent in all the great holy writings of the world, and that myth then can become a guiding force in our daily living. For example, I had an epic dream in 1982, and while reading *Hero with a Thousand Faces* years later, in 1990, the book walked lock step with that dream. I was paying attention.

Early in the interview, when asked by Moyer about the best way to discover the power of myth, Campbell replied, "Follow your bliss." This quote was mostly misunderstood, as many thought he was referring to hedonism, and assumed him to be talking about sexual bliss. If you read the rest of Campbell's works, however, you find that not to be his intent at all. Campbell was instead saying, "If your life is ever going to have any meaning and purpose, you are going to have to find the thing you enjoy doing most and do that as often as possible." To follow your bliss, according to Campbell, is to find enjoyment and make it your lifelong quest, much like the heroes of myths around the world.

Several years ago, my wife and I were at a Sunday evening service at our local church. The pastor, an excellent preacher, incidentally delivered that night a 15-minute devotional sermon. Those 15 minutes changed our lives. Rev. Scott's sermon that night described the story of the children of Israel in the wilderness, and how God sent them every day to gather manna. They were told to gather today what you need for today, not to gather today for tomorrow because God would provide every day. Furthermore, the manna became wormy and inedible if kept overnight for the next day. At one point the pastor asked us, "Have you ever wondered why God would make the manna rancid if it was kept for another day? Do you think God did that to punish them in some way? No! He did it so that the children would have to go out and get their good stuff every single day. Now, you need to find out what your good stuff is, and go and find it every day."

For both of us, that little sermon was a rather immediate revelation into the amount of time that we were wasting—a lot of minutes, hours, days, and weeks, saying things and doing things that were basically meaningless to us, and that we needed to find our "good stuff" and begin living our lives involved in those things. For an altruist such as myself, that's not an easy thing. My "good stuff" is usually sublimated in your good stuff. If you're happy, I'm happy. If you're pleased with me, then I'm pleased with me. Unfortunately, the reciprocal of that is also true. If you're upset (with me), then I'm upset too. What did I do wrong? How can I make it right? Will you forgive me? Fortunately, somewhere along the way, my wife introduced me to a way of thinking and the basic concept is this: "What somebody says to you or about you says more about them than it does about you." Finding my "good stuff" totally separate from your good stuff has been a lifelong adventure in self-discovery.

Now my good stuff is primarily time in my own home—time with my wife, my computer, or with a good book, or in conversation with relatives or good friends. My good stuff involves reading and writing, most often with a cup of coffee or tea. But my good stuff also involves trips to Indiana to watch my granddaughter play basketball, to California to visit with my son and daughter-in-law, or to Chattanooga Valley to spend time with good friends. My "good stuff" involves a deepening relationship with Wakan Tanka (or God, if you prefer), my guiding force in everything I do. My good stuff has included continuing to read the published works of Joseph Campbell. My good stuff is boiled down to three words—life is good.

Your good stuff is not a luxury. It's necessary—like breathing and having a pulse. It keeps you going on days when nothing around you is going right and nobody appreciates what you do. Your good stuff not only saves your life, but also radiates to the world to help save all of us.

"Follow your bliss," Joseph Campbell told me in 1987. More than 30 years later, I am still learning what that means. But as I seek life, liberty, and the pursuit of happiness, I'm following my bliss.

[1] "Joseph Campbell and The Power of Myth," https://billmoyers.com/series/joseph-campbell-and-the-power-of-myth-1988/

Two Things God Overdid

Okay, hear me out before you pass judgment on me. Cain argued with God about his punishment for killing his brother. Moses questioned God on a number of occasions regarding His care and feeding of the Israelites on their journey to the Promised Land. Job, especially, questioned God regarding the severity of his distress.

So, in a long line of saints and sinners, I am going to question God. Although I am pretty impressed with God's creation and the way He runs things in general, there are a couple of things that I think He got a little carried away with. The two things are odors and pain.

Regarding odors, it is my opinion that odors serve two basic functions: one is to say, "Don't touch this," and the other is to say, "Under no circumstances should you eat this." Why else does something need to smell so bad? But when you think about it, don't things smell worse than they need to in order to accomplish these two things? Couldn't certain things smell less than half as bad as they do and you still not want to eat them? I don't have to be graphic for you to understand what I'm saying. You've had a baby, a dog, a teenager, or a husband. You understand.

But the thing, I think, God overdid the most is pain. Again, the only good thing pain does in my opinion is to tell us that something is wrong and needs attention. When I think about how bad something hurts, I've got to wonder if it is absolutely necessary for the pain to be so excruciatingly painful. Wouldn't it get my attention if it were half that bad or a fourth that bad? Consider a toothache. Consider back problems. Consider a headache. What does a headache tell you but "take aspirin"? It could tell you that you have a brain tumor, but that is probably not the case. Maybe it could tell you to get your eyes checked. But most people have none of these problems; their head just hurts. In the case of a migraine, it hurts really badly.

The worst pain I ever had was lower back pain. It was so bad I couldn't walk; I couldn't even stand up straight. Do you know how it started? It started with a sneeze. I was trying to keep a cup of coffee from sloshing, and I turned my head and torso to keep from sneezing in someone's face. That's when lightning struck my lower back. I almost ended up in the hospital, but a physical therapist helped me get my pain under control. But the second most intense pain was even more dramatic. You might want to bite down on something. To prep me to have my big toenail removed, with no warning whatsoever, the doctor stuck a needle under my toenail. Under the nail! I nearly passed out. He smiled and said, "I didn't feel a thing." Well, I can assure you that I did. So God, "Why does the quick around our nails need to be so sensitive? If it was a third as sensitive, I promise not to stick anything in it. I promise not to pull them off." And all of this only refers to physical pain. What about emotional pain, such as loss and grief? The Bee Gees sang, "How do you mend a broken heart?" and the question lingers still. When our hearts hurt, there is sometimes no consolation. God, was that necessary?

Why do we need to hurt so badly? The Greek root word for pain means "to pay or to punish." To pay for what? To be punished for what?

The pain industry is in the billions of dollars a year. When you consider all the pain medication and therapies that are used to ease pain, it is really staggering in its scope. So does God let us hurt this badly to create all that GDP? I kind of doubt it, but what could it be? On that great and terrible day when I stand before my Maker, I'm going to walk right up to God and ask, "God, why did things on Earth need to smell so bad? And why did we need to hurt so much? And while we're at it, why did you make rattlesnakes?" Then shall God say unto me, "Do you prefer smoking or non-smoking?"

The Angel

As my wife and I were leaving the theater after seeing *Slumdog Millionaire*, these words popped in my head, "Man's evil is surpassed only by his goodness." I put it in quotes because I feel like I'm quoting myself.

I am constantly amazed at how cruel man can be to man. I am astonished at how mean and hateful people can be to each other, even to members of their own family. People rob, kill, and torture for little or nothing. Some people kill for the sheer pleasure of killing. They actually enjoy inflicting pain and suffering on other people. But at the same time, I am constantly amazed at how good people can be to each other. These people are good not only to family and friends, but are good to perfect strangers. People sacrifice life and limb to help someone in distress, many times for people they don't even know.

Many years ago, when I left my house to go to work, it was pouring down rain. I worked in the financial services industry, so I had on a business suit. As soon as I turned from our subdivision onto a busy road, I had a flat tire. I pulled off the road to decide what to do. I didn't have AAA, but it didn't matter because there were no cell phones then. I considered my options and none of them were good. Before I could trouble my mind, out of nowhere, a truck pulled up and parked behind me. The driver approached my window. I rolled it down and said hello. This man standing in the rain asked, "May I help you with your tire?" I replied, "I hate to ask you to do that in the pouring rain." He said, "You didn't ask. I'm on my way home from work and am already dirty; there's no reason for both of us to get wet." So I sat in the car while this complete stranger changed my tire. I didn't carry much cash then and all I had in my wallet was a five- dollar bill. When he came to my window to tell me he was finished, I thanked him warmly and handed him the money, apologizing that it was so little. He said, "I didn't want any money; I just wanted to help." He got back in his truck and drove away. I never even knew his name.

Over the years, as I've thought about this encounter, I've wondered if he was an angel. It was just a bit freaky how he appeared out of nowhere, changed the tire, and disappeared. No introductions. No lifetime friendship. No nothing. But then I remember the time about a year later when I stopped in the very same spot and helped a stranded family from California. Since it was hot summertime, I even invited them to wait in our home until they could get help. I try to be a good person, but I'm no angel. It is my pleasure to help other people if there is any way I can. So regarding the man who helped me, this is what I think happened. A very kind man on his way home from work saw a motorist in need. It was his pleasure to help me. I realize now that the money was the least of his concerns. He probably gave it away.

"Man's evil is surpassed only by his goodness." May the tribe of those who want to help each other increase. May those who only want to help be multiplied by thousands. May man's evil always be overcome by his goodness.

The Lizard Way

> "When the lotus opened I didn't notice and went away
>   empty-handed
> Only now and again do I suddenly sit up from my dreams
> To smell a strange fragrance.
> It comes on the south wind,
> A vague hint that makes me ache with longing,
> Like the eager breath of summer waiting to be completed.
> I didn't know what was so near, or that it was mine.
> This perfect sweetness blossoming in the depths of my
>   heart."[1]

My grandfather bought the house a few years before I was born. Unfortunately, he also died a few years before I was born. I never knew my maternal grandfather.

He bought the house in Laguna Beach, Florida, from two elderly sisters. He simply knocked on the door and asked them if they had ever considered selling the house. He loaded them in his car, drove them to Panama City, where he gave them about two thousand dollars, and they gave him the deed to their house.

Most of my earliest memories take place in that house and that beach. Even though, after a few additions, the house would comfortably sleep twenty people, we called it "the beach cottage" or just "the cottage." Since the house was only 90 miles due south of my hometown of Enterprise, Alabama, we spent quite a bit of time there. Most of the time I was with my immediate family, but many times we were joined by my grandmother, my aunts and uncles, and my cousins on my mother's side of the family. The house sits right on Highway 98, which runs along the Gulf of Mexico for several hundred miles. To get to the beach from the house, we only needed to walk out the front door, cross 98, and walk down "our" path to the beach. This path wound its way through the dunes to the beach. Except for this path, the dunes were covered with shrubs, sea oats, brambles, broken beer bottles, and a wide assortment of other hazards so we really had no option but to stay on the path. Only God knows the miles I trekked down and back up that path of sand.

We could actually see the gulf over the dunes and hear the surf from our front porch. As a child, the porch was only a place to play board games with my cousins, but as I got older I learned to enjoy just sitting, drinking iced tea, listening to the surf, and watching pelicans lazily glide by. From there I had a bird's eye view of schools of dolphins as they made their way through the blue gulf waters to destinations unknown.

My memories of that house and that beach are some of the richest memories of my life. I never enjoyed being with my own family as much as I did being with them there. My dad, who could be quite stern and severe at times, would relax and show his lighter side. My mother made sure we had all of what we needed and most of what we wanted. My brother, sister, and I enjoyed each other's company as well. Our daily routine usually included getting up early to eat "beach toast" (slightly overdone with puddles of butter and fig preserves). Then we immediately headed down to the beach, where we played for hours. Around 11 a.m., when it got too hot to stay in the sun, we would walk back up the path to the cottage. Climbing that path after hours in the surf and sand was hard work. My legs felt as if they were made of rubber and lead. It was worth the effort, as Mother would feed us tomato sandwiches, watermelon, cantaloupe, and fresh peaches. For dessert, she would give us homemade chocolate cake or pecan pie. Then it was time for a nap. When we got old enough, Mother let us walk down the road to the Seahorse, where we played pinball. These were the ones with real balls, real flippers, and all sorts of lights and sounds. Vegas can't hold a candle to the machines we played! We played for as long as we had a dime in our pockets.

At about 4 p.m., we would put our swimsuits back on and head back down to the beach. As a kid, it was another fun time. As an adult, it became a sacred time. As those beach afternoons melted into evening, it took the sun an eternity to finally disappear into the water. When the tide was out, you could almost walk to Mexico. We dug for crabs, made drip castles, and many times just watched the blazing ball of fire slowly sink into the Gulf of Mexico. When it was too dark to ring out another minute, we made the long, tired trip up the path, through the dunes to the cottage. There, MeMama had prepared a southern feast with plenty of sweet tea to wash it down. After dinner, we played board games and, if we were lucky, my aunt would take us to Miracle Strip, Goofy Golf, or to ride the go-carts.

Once a year, usually around the 4th of July, the entire Redmon clan descended on the beach house for a weekend of fun. Being with all my Redmon relatives there was like heaven on earth. I remember so many things about those weekends, but it's the laughter I remember the most. Everything was funny. We did all the normal "beach" things, and in addition, my uncle Herbert always brought a boat from his shop in Enterprise. He took all of us who wanted to go to Phillip's Inlet to ski. We would ski from mid-afternoon until it was almost too dark to see. At dusk, when the lake was calm as glass, the skis would sing beneath our feet.

When I was about 18 years old, to accommodate beach goers from surrounding homes and developments, somebody plowed a new path to the water about 20 yards west of our path. Our family, as well as scores of other people, started using that path. It was much wider and less cluttered with undergrowth. For many years, I continued to use the old family trail. Many times in the early morning, I would pour a cup of coffee, cross the street, and take the old path to the shore. Since by now we shared that path with a number of small creatures, my three-year-old son started calling it "the lizard way." One particular morning, when he was up early, he asked if he could walk down with me and of course I told him he could. He enjoyed the trip and I appreciated the company. With a cup of hot coffee in my left hand and my son in tow on my right, we made our trek down the hill toward the beach. When we got about halfway down the path, he looked up at me and asked, "Dad, why do you always want to go the lizard way?" That was thirty-five years ago and I still don't know the answer. I'm sure it had to do with the fact that I knew that path that those two old women and my grandfather had blazed would soon be gone. I also knew that someday that house, too, would be gone. Or at least gone to us. In 1992, for reasons only they knew, my mother and her sister sold the house to complete strangers. None of us were in the position to buy it, so after forty-five years in the Redmon family, the cottage belonged to someone else.

During the summer of 2008, my wife, our son and his wife, our four-month-old granddaughter, and several of our son's friends took a vacation to Laguna Beach, Florida. Our rental house was less than a mile from the old family beach house. Approaching the house, I looked for my old path, but there was no evidence a path had ever been there. It was a path for crabs and lizards only. At the road was a sign at the new path that read, "Private beach. Owners only." What about people who owned it for forty-five years, can we use it?

The "lizard way" has become a metaphor for any path in my life that I try to keep open. Instead of using my feet, I use the telephone, the mailbox, email, texts, and as many face-to-face occasions as possible to keep those paths open. I never knew Burt Redmon, but I think that he would have been proud of me for understanding the significance of his house and his winding path to the beach. I can't ever walk that path again, but I will always treasure the memory of that morning when my little boy asked me, "Dad, why do you always want to go the lizard way?" I'm not sure. Give me a few more years and I'll figure it out.

[1]Rabindranath Tagore, "I Didn't Know," in *The Soul in Love*, ed. Deepak Chopra (New York: Harmony Books, 2001), 96.

Death Be Not Proud

My wife and I used to walk together. A lot. We usually walked at Chickamauga Park, a Civil War battlefield near our home, but at other times when we were in no particular hurry, we would drive to downtown Chattanooga, Tennessee, not far from our home. We would park on one end of town, walk the length of the city, cross the pedestrian bridge over the Tennessee River, make a lap around Coolidge Park and back to our car. It's about a four-mile walk and would take about an hour, and was a route offering beautiful scenery as well as an excellent aerobic workout.

On one particular afternoon, a car pulled up to a red light as if it was going to stop. As a general rule, drivers are courteous and would let us cross, but I had an uneasy feeling about walking in front of this one. We stopped, as it lurched forward and made a right turn. It wasn't a close call by any means, and nobody was injured, but it was me paying attention to the car instead of the driver paying attention to us. It always pays to be aware of cars if you're walking.

Back in October of 1991, I was on my way to attend a funeral service at Lane Funeral Home in Rossville, Georgia. On my way, I made a stop to do some banking business in Fort Oglethorpe. I parked at the bank, walked across the parking lot, went into the bank, and completed my transaction. As I walked out of the bank to return to my car, I was distracted by someone in a passing car on a side street and thinking that it was someone that I knew, wanted to offer a friendly wave. I was looking to my right instead of watching what I was doing. About the time I figured out that the person in the passing car was not my friend, I found myself airborne. My body turned sideways in the air so that I fell prone on the trunk of a car. I rolled off the back of the car and onto the asphalt. At that point, the car's rear tire stopped about three inches from my head. I got up from the ground and dusted myself off as a woman got out of her car to see if I was okay. She was as white as a sheet, which left me wondering if SHE was okay! I assured her that I was fine, and she returned to her car and drove away. That's the last I ever saw of her. Later, as I pieced together what happened, I figured out that she was backing out of a parking space at a rapid rate of speed and didn't see me walk out of the bank. I wasn't looking either and didn't see her coming. She clipped me with her bumper, which propelled me into the air and onto the trunk of her car. I was literally inches and a fraction of a second from serious injury or death.

I went into the bank and told my friend John, the bank president, what had just occurred in case someone else told him about the incident. As a matter of precaution, he encouraged me to get checked out at a nearby hospital, but I assured him that I was fine, and went on my way. So what did I do? What else could I do? I went to the funeral! When I got to the service, I found a phone and called my wife to tell her about the incident.

> Me: Guess what just happened to me?
> Her: No idea.
> Me: I just got hit by a car!
> Her: How bad? Is the car totaled?
> Me: The car didn't get hit by a car. I got hit by a car!
> Her: Oh, so sorry! Are you okay?
> Me: Yeah, I'm fine.
> Her: Where are you?
> Me: I'm at Lane's Funeral Home.

It was at that point that my legs started shaking and my stomach started shaking, and I started trembling from head to toe. I began to shake uncontrollably. I told my wife that I would have to call her back. I ended the call and allowed several minutes to pass while I composed myself before going into the chapel.

Several years later, I shared my story with a Vietnam vet, and he said, "You had the combat shakes!" And what is that? "It's what you get when the man in the fox hole beside you takes a bullet and you know that it could just as easily have been you. That's the combat shakes." Yep. For sure. I had the combat shakes.

Not many people get to attend their own funeral, and I feel very fortunate that I was one of the living attending a funeral that day. Since that day, I have never failed to yield the right of way to automobiles when I am a pedestrian. I do not assume that they are going to stop. I never assume that they are going to let me walk in front of them. I don't assume anything. I just pay attention to what they're doing and assume that they are not paying attention to me.

So can I claim that I nearly died when all I really felt was a little soreness from the fall? Only God knows. I do know that a few nights later, I had a dream that was something like a near-death experience, and that for weeks I had a heightened awareness of everything around me. There's nothing like a potential brush with death to give you a deep appreciation for living. The grass is greener, the sky is bluer, and birds sing more loudly. The ordinary is suddenly extraordinary. Regrettably, that sensation wears off over time. The reality is that everything is still extraordinary. We just stop seeing it.

I have a good friend who used to live across the street from a funeral home. He said that people would often ask him if it bothered him to wake up in the mornings and see a funeral home. His reply was always, "No, it would bother me to wake up and look across the street and see my house!"

Cheque, Please

A Facebook friend posted on her status yesterday that she had gotten her driver's license renewed, and had encountered problems with the DMV. In a flash of memory that I have successfully suppressed for a number of years, my problem with the DMV came roaring to the surface.

Back in 1984, we lived in Rossville, Georgia, a small town near Chattanooga, Tennessee. We lived way back in the sticks, off of Mission Ridge Road. It was a bit of a drive just to get to the starting place of getting somewhere else.

Lafayette, Georgia, was, and still is, the county seat of Walker County. At that time, all official business happened in Lafayette. It's pronounced Luh FAY ette, and was named for the French General Marquis de LaFayette, which of course is pronounced Lah fay ETTE. I don't remember ever going to Lafayette for any fun reason, though I'm sure that if you happen to live there it's a wonderful place. I just never found that side of the town. Going to Lafayette was typically just pure drudgery. Now, years later, there is a nice four-lane highway from Rossville to the county seat. At that time it was a two-lane road, about a 35-minute drive from our house, depending on traffic, and you could always count on traffic. You could usually count on a few really slow-moving cars or a tractor, and there weren't many opportunities to pass. I avoid going to Lafayette however possible.

This particular year, I had waited until the last day to renew my driver's license. These days, living in Catoosa County, we renew our licenses by mail, but those were different times and we had to show up in person at the DMV to renew. I got together everything I needed—the renewal notice, current driver's license, and checkbook—and headed to Lafayette. I don't remember specific traffic situations of course, but I can tell you that it wasn't smooth sailing. It just never was. There were always traffic obstacles. It always took a l-o-n-g time to get to Lafayette, Georgia.

When I finally arrived at the Walker County branch of the Georgia DMV, it took me a few minutes to find a place to park. I looked up and the line was out the door. I hadn't expected that kind of wait and hadn't taken anything to read to keep me company. This wasn't the dark ages, but it was before the days of iPods, Blackberries, or cell phones, so handy for twittering away the time. Not the dark ages, but much darker than it is now. Since I didn't have many options, I say, "Don't you just enjoy watching people?" For me, the answer is no. I didn't then and I still don't.

Finally, after waiting for an hour or more of what I thought to be pure agony, it was my turn at the window. The nice lady asked for my documentation and I handed it to her. She smiled and told me my exact total, and I opened my checkbook to complete the transaction. I opened the checkbook cover, and to my complete horror, realized that I didn't have one single, solitary check. I just looked at her and she politely looked back at me. I looked again. "Please, God! I just need ONE!!" But no, I did not have one single check. At this point, I considered my choices. I could beg her to renew my license without payment and promise to put the check in the mail first thing tomorrow. Probably not. I could fall down on the floor, beat my hands and kick my feet, screaming about what a bad hand life had dealt me. The jail was only a couple of blocks away, so decided against that option. I could get out of line, walk to my car, drive back to Rossville, Georgia, get a check, and drive back to Luh FAY ette, and stand in line for another hour to renew my license. I decided that, as awful as it sounded, it was probably the best option. So I did. I walked to my car, drove for 35 minutes back to my house, picked up a new bundle of checks, walked back to my car and drove to Lafayette, Georgia. I got behind at least 14 slow drivers, and at least six tractors—maybe it was 16 tractors—I don't remember. When I finally got back to the DMV, I parked my car and walked inside. I had come prepared this time, armed with a good book, and I took my place once again at the back of the line, prepared for another long wait. I had stood there for about 15 minutes when the very nice lady saw me and motioned me forward to her window. She explained to the person who was next in line that I had already waited in line once, and he didn't seem to mind letting me move ahead. She smiled and told me again the amount of payment that was needed. I smiled back, handed her my documentation and wrote a check. Wow. Déjà vu. Weird.

I read recently that most of the lessons we learn in life we learn too late to be of much use. I understand what that writer had in mind—that it often seems many of life's lessons come at great cost and involve a lot of pain, but it's too late to do anything about it. And many times that is the case. But I can tell you that this particular lesson didn't come too late for me. I have never shown up anywhere at any time for any reason without a method of payment. Nada. Never. Not once. For that matter, I usually have more than one method of payment. "Let's see. Can I give you a check? Debit card? Visa? American Express? Bank draft? If you prefer, I can just debit the home equity line of credit, or heck, here's the deed to my house!"

For years, we traveled to Lafayette quite often. Our granddaughter lived there. Only it's in Indiana, and it's pronounced Lah fay ETTE, like the general. It was 1,008 miles round trip, and the drive was no problem at all. We did it in a weekend.

We, the Living

"The trees that have it in their pent-up buds
To darken nature and be summer woods
Let them think twice before they use their powers
To blot out and drink up and sweep away
These flowery waters and these watery flowers
From snow that melted only yesterday."[1]

In 1990 and 1991, I lost several people who were significant in my life. The cumulative losses were almost devastating to me. There is no way to say that one was more important than another, because each of them held a special place in my life and heart. But when my good friend Geoff Hood died, I thought that I would surely die as well. Geoff and his fiancé, Molly Larue, were fulfilling a lifelong dream and through hiking the Appalachian Trail when they were brutally murdered by a madman. I didn't have the capacity to absorb the loss of Geoff and his friendship, but a sustaining help to me then and now is my continued and deep friendship with his mother and sister.

In May of 1991, Geoff's mother asked me to accompany them to New Bloomfield, Pennsylvania, and be present for the trial of Paul David Crews, who had been indicted in their murders. I was honored to be able to do that, but was totally unprepared. I had once sat on a jury in the trial of sister vs. sister, fighting over a headstone for a family grave, and thought that was bad. This one was a totally different situation.

The facts of the case are as follows: Geoff and Molly were spending the night at the official halfway point of the trail, the Thelma Marks Shelter near Duncannon, Pennsylvania. On the evening of September 11, 1990, Paul David Crews, traveling northbound, hiked into the shelter and apparently shared a meal with Geoff and Molly. Early the next morning while they slept, he shot Geoff three times with a .22 revolver and left him to die. He then tied Molly with tent rope, raped and tortured her, and slit her throat with a hunting knife. He then took most of their gear and headed southbound on the trail. He was arrested one week later at Harper's Ferry, West Virginia.

All the evidence against Crews was circumstantial. There were no eyewitnesses to the murder. On the morning of September 12, however, Biff and Cindi Bowen were on the trail about 50 feet up from the shelter when he sensed something wasn't right. He walked down the hill to the shelter where he found the mutilated bodies. This trial, which lasted a week, was the first DNA trial in the state of Pennsylvania. This evidence, and the testimony of the hikers, was crucial to the conviction of Paul Crews. Upon his conviction, he was sentenced to be put to death. I had long held the political opinion that the death penalty was inhumane, but that day I felt differently. Finally, after 15 years of appeals, in 2006, Paul David Crews' sentence was commuted to two life sentences with no chance of parole. I was in the courtroom the day of that decision. For years, I had felt that death was too good a fate for him. Now seeing him, I could no longer continue to hate him. Prison had taken its toll, and he was just a pathetic old man.

During the trial, we all dealt with our anger and stress in a variety of ways. One of the things that I did was to get up early, usually around sunrise, and jog several miles. I found that pounding the pavement was therapeutic for me. In New Bloomfield, you don't have to jog far out of town to be "in the country." I always took the same easterly route out of town, and about a mile out, I would pass a field where horses were grazing. Every morning they would come over to the fence to greet me, and I would stop to rub their noses and help them greet the day. On one particular morning, however, I decided to run to the opposite end of town. On my return, a deep, clear puddle got my attention and I stopped for a closer look. It was just a large puddle, but clear as a spring. There was some green life growing in the water, but there were also two or three empty beer cans at the bottom. As I resumed my jog, I thought about all the life in that puddle of water—billions of microscopic organisms, hydrozoa, mitochondria, and amoeba—a myriad of tiny creatures that jetted and darted, filling the water with energy. When I got back to the B&B where we were staying, I wrote a poem about that little roadside pool. I have lost the poem, but I remember bits and pieces of it. It referred to the beer cans as "remnants of Friday night laughter," and concluded with, "There is more life in you than all the death in the world."

I read my poem that morning at breakfast. Molly's mother later asked me, "David, did you have any way of knowing about Molly's fascination with microscopic organisms, amoeba in particular?" I assured her that I did not. I just know that on that particular morning, a roadside puddle helped me to deal with the courtroom, and continues to help me to consider the sustaining power of the natural world around us, often in the things we cannot see.

On Mother's Day in May of 1991, I hiked that part of the trail from Duncannon to the Thelma Marks Shelter, along with Geoff's mother and sister. It was one of the most peaceful experiences of my life. The shelter has since been torn down, and we attended the dedication of the new shelter. I experienced the same serenity that day as the first time I was there. For me it is a sanctified place.

There is one thing that I learned in the year of my grief that I have never forgotten. Of all the things that you can do to help yourself through great loss, there is one thing you must do—you must survive.

[1]Robert Frost, *New Enlarged Anthology of Robert Frost Poems* (Spring Pools: Washington Square Press,1970),185.

Code Word— Mountain Dew

This afternoon, I was in a department store making a return for my wife. I wasn't really paying much attention to the transaction going on with the customer in front of me, until the sales clerk said, "The Mountain Dew is four thirty-eight." That's what she said. "The Mountain Dew is four thirty-eight." She spoke plain English and was not hard to understand. I understood exactly what she said and she said, "The Mountain Dew is four thirty-eight." This store sold clothing, not groceries, so I thought this to be quite odd. I know that many stores have coolers for soft drinks, but not this department store. Furthermore, I was now looking at the purchase of the customer in front of me, and it was a single item of clothing and not a soft drink. Also, isn't $4.38 a lot of money for a Mountain Dew, no matter where?

As I continued to ponder the transaction, I decided that perhaps the two of them were speaking in code. Maybe they are lovers, and the translation is: "I'll see you at 4:38 in the usual place." Or perhaps, "Bet $438 on Mountain Dew tonight at the track." Or maybe they are members of an international drug cartel and she was saying, "We'll drop 438 kilos at the mountain drop point early Saturday morning." Perhaps the cashier is a CIA operative and the customer is a Russian spy and they were communicating that 438 million would be transferred to the Cayman Island account by noon tomorrow. Even worse, maybe they were saying, "Take care of all four of them with the .38!"

Whatever the meaning, I'm no fool, and I knew something big was going down. Was I supposed to call the police? Should I just look the other way? What was I supposed to do? I had seen it in movies, but I had never been in this situation in real life.

As it neared my turn at the register, I wondered if I was being watched—if I would somehow unwittingly be dragged into their net, their little plan. Would I ever see my wife and child again? Giving the words, "the Mountain Dew is four thirty-eight," one last spin in my head before it was my turn to deal with this woman; the full weight of what she had said began to sink in. It came to me clearly, and I knew exactly what she had said. I knew exactly what I had to do. "The amount due is four thirty-eight."

Exit 296

My wife and I were in Atlanta recently to attend a wedding. Any time we go to Atlanta, we travel down I-75 and pass Exit 296, the Cassville-White exit. I've never been to Cassville or White, but I've stopped at that exit many times. The Waffle House at that exit holds special memories for both of us.

After high school graduation and a careful search, our son enrolled at Georgia Tech in Atlanta. I was proud then that he made the cut to be accepted there, and I'm still proud. When The Georgia Institute of Technology comes up in conversation, I don't hesitate to say, "My son graduated from that college!" In a lot of ways, I think I enjoyed the Tech experience more than he did. As a matter of fact, he says, "Dad, you don't enjoy Georgia Tech. You just go there." I'm sure that's true to a great extent. For him, it was long and arduous, but we thoroughly enjoyed our visits to Atlanta and the campus for his five years there. The first couple of years, we held season tickets and enjoyed the football games and being around college kids again. We enjoyed getting to know the young Tech graduate and his family who held adjacent seats, and we were excited for the possibilities available for those who survived.

My fondest memories of his college life, however, were my meetings with him and whatever group of friends he brought along for the ride, when we would connect at the Waffle House at Exit 296. That exit, Cassville-White, is almost an exact halfway point between his dorm and our house. It took all parties about 45–55 minutes to get there, and it became a great meeting spot. We used it for handing off items he would occasionally need from home, or for him to hand off items he wanted to return. Most often, though, it became a place of serendipity—the never planned, spur of the moment, late night call asking if we wanted to meet for eggs and waffles. We were typically in bed, often asleep, when the phone would ring. I knew who it was and what he wanted. Within 15 minutes or so, I would be headed down I-75 south, occasionally convincing my wife to join us. Arriving around 11p.m. or so, we ate, talked, laughed (mostly laughed), until around 1 a.m., and then I headed home and back to bed by 2 or 2:30 a.m.

My son usually brought one or more of his friends along for these outings—as a single child, he found brothers and sisters everywhere he went, so we never knew what group would show up for these rendezvous. Occasionally, he would come alone, but there were times when six or seven or eight of us would gather in the Waffle House booth and laugh and talk until the wee hours of the morning. The night I remember most vividly was a cold winter night, and it was just the two of us. Our son was dressed in jeans, sweatshirt, and his green toboggan, a most prized possession. After we talked for a while and our food arrived, he got a big cheesy grin on his face, and pulled off his hat to reveal a very bald head. The grin remained for a few seconds while he held the hat over his shaved smooth head, giving me opportunity to admire the new cut. I laughed and laughed. I don't remember what was so funny about it all, but it was just funny. I don't remember if he had lost a bet or what, but in the dead middle of winter, he'd had his hair completely shaved off. I can't recall one single detail about the rest of that night, but remember vividly his green hat and shaved head.

I know the dangers of looking back to past experiences as "the best of times," because the best of times are always ahead of us. What we have now and what we will have is all that really matters. Even though that Waffle House is long gone, when I drive past Exit 296, I remember fondly and longingly those special nights when we would be jolted out of bed and find ourselves headed south to meet our boy at the Waffle House. So many times I have not realized the magnitude of a moment until years later. In the case of Cassville-White, I savored every minute, knowing that it would end. I tried to memorize the faces and record the laughter. I knew that those days (nights) were numbered. These meetings are now years in the rear view mirror, but the pleasure I received from those midnight encounters hasn't diminished.

In the movie, *Saving Private Ryan*, the last words of the film are of Pvt. Ryan asking his wife if he had lived good enough—had he lived a life that deserved the sacrifices that had been made on his behalf. She assured him that he had indeed honored their sacrifice. I don't always live good enough. I don't always pay attention. But I was paying attention at Exit 296, and pay attention every time I drive past there even now.

But here's the thing: If I missed something very important yesterday, the most important thing to know is not "Woe is me, how could I have missed that?" but rather, "Am I living good enough today? Am I paying attention today?" If you're still beating yourself up about what you missed yesterday, you're not living today.

My Magic Rock

I grew up in Enterprise, Alabama, a small town in the southeast corner of the state. Just to say "Enterprise, Alabama" gives me a good feeling. I was born there, and except for a year in Atmore, I lived there until I left for college at the age of 19. I never returned there to live. I've only made short visits with my family over the years. I haven't lived there for more than 30 years, but I still call Enterprise my home. Among the many special virtues of that little town, Enterprise is actually famous. Right in the dead center of town stands the world famous Boll Weevil Monument. Now, you may be thinking, if it's "world famous," why have I never heard of it? Well, now you have! But please don't take my word for it—Google it! In the late 1800s, the money crop in that part of Alabama and surrounding areas was cotton. In the early 1900s, the boll weevil came from Mexico across Texas, Louisiana, and Mississippi, into Alabama, destroying acres and acres of cotton along the way. The boll weevil was responsible for the devastation of crops in and around Enterprise.

Although I don't have 100 percent assurance that it happened exactly this way, it's pretty close. Salvation came in the form of George Washington Carver, the famous scientist from the Tuskegee Institute. Dr. Carver tested the soil and suggested that the farmers consider growing peanuts instead of cotton. Local cotton farmers H.M. Sessions and C.W. Baston took his advice and thus began the peanut dynasty in Coffee County, Alabama. In order to thank the boll weevil for forcing this good fortune on them, the city erected a monument in the middle of town. Worldwide, people have told this story to illustrate triumph from despair. On March 1, 2007, a powerful tornado ripped through town, leveling entire neighborhoods, destroying the high school where I lived my teenage years, and killing eight students. The city again erected a memorial, this time to remember those students, once again digging deep to find triumph from despair. Enterprise had recovered before, and it would recover again.

But about the Boll Weevil Monument—I don't recommend driving much out of your way to see it. Unfortunately, it is only a replica of the original, and a shadow of its former glory. Vandals and rival football teams have ripped the large bug out of the lady's hands many times over the years, and in the late 1990s, a large portion of the monument was destroyed and the city decided that it could not be repaired. I miss the original statue, but I still make a point to drive past her every time I go to Enterprise.

I still have part ownership in a piece of property in Enterprise, having inherited it from my parents, and my grandfather before them. It has been farmland, peanut land, and a number of other things. About five years ago while walking the property with my family, I reached down and picked up an ordinary garden-variety rock, and put it in my pocket. The rock looks like nothing special at all, but if you look closely (and want to see it), you can see in its shape and markings a look somewhat like a snake's head. I hate snakes, so that really doesn't have much significance to me, but I keep my rock with me in my pocket all the time. Over the years, its value to me has changed and grown. It has become, in a word, my prayer rock. Quite often when I reach into my pocket for my keys or loose change, I handle the rock, and I pray for my brother and sister, and for the welfare of our inheritance. I pray for their protection, and that the three of us will be good stewards of what has been passed down to our care. When I take time to be conscious of it, I pray for much more, praying the prayer that Jesus taught us to pray.

Before you decide that having a prayer rock is strange, consider that it's similar to praying the rosary, an exercise practiced by millions of people worldwide every day. Praying the rosary follows a pattern, which is repeated over and over, sometimes several times a day. I could carry rosary beads, but I just carry my rock. Besides, rosary beads don't come from Enterprise, Alabama. Furthermore, even though my beliefs and faith have morphed significantly over the years, I hold to my childhood rock solid belief that prayer changes things. I know that, at least, it changes me.

No, I don't actually believe that this rock is a talisman; there's nothing magic about it. It's just an ordinary rock that I picked up in an ordinary field in an ordinary town in south Alabama. I do, however, believe that the reminder it evokes for me is very real.

There's a lovely book by Annie Dillard, *Teaching a Stone to Talk*, and the book cover says that Dillard "explores the world of natural facts and human meanings." I may never teach my stone to talk, but it has certainly taught me to pray.

Caution: Horses

This afternoon I was driving down an interstate highway that I frequently use, and I found myself following a horse trailer. On the back, in very large letters, was the warning: CAUTION: HORSES. Over the years, I've seen this warning from time to time, especially when show horses are being transported. But these were regular, garden-variety horses. Personally, I am not a horse enthusiast, but I admire them and appreciate their grandeur and beauty. As a matter of fact, my girlfriend from my junior high school days had a couple of horses—Smoky and Blue Boy. I remember enjoying my time riding those horses all over her farm in Enterprise, Alabama. If memory serves me correctly, Smoky was an Arabian and Blue Boy was an Appaloosa. They were gorgeous, remarkable animals. Norma usually rode Blue Boy and I rode the tamer Smoky, but the more we rode, I built confidence so we would trade horses from time to time. I learned to enjoy the thrill of the full gallop and the smoothness of the canter. I not only enjoyed riding them, but I enjoyed feeding and grooming as well. Perhaps for those few years, I was an enthusiast after all. They were fun years, and I learned to appreciate the horses.

I've never been quite sure, however, what the caution sign on the back of horse trailers actually means. Does it mean: "Please don't ram this trailer"? Does it mean that these animals are so valuable that you need to slow down, and pass with care? Does the warning serve to remind that the animals are just so fragile, that if you blow your horn they will try to bolt or stampede? Maybe it just means to "stay back, please." Seems like a good possibility to me! And then, there's the CAUTION: SHOW HORSES sign. Now, do I assume that these animals are even more valuable than garden-variety horses and that I should be even more careful than when approaching non-show horses? Does all of this serve to remind me that, even if I don't value my car or my life, that I should at least value your horses?

It occurs to me, though, that we might need a sign in our back windows or a bumper sticker that reads CAUTION: PEOPLE. The closest I've seen to that is the "Baby on Board" bumper sticker. Now this one used to puzzle me as well, until I realized that it serves as a sign to alert emergency personnel that there is a child in the car, in case of a catastrophic accident when the driver may be incapacitated or worse. That makes good sense, but perhaps we should take it further and post the sign that says CAUTION: PEOPLE. Maybe a driver will see it and be just a bit more careful, a bit more courteous, and a little more attentive because he knows for a fact that there are people in the car; people whose lives are important and valuable.

Taking this all one step further, maybe we need to imagine a stamp on the forehead of every person we meet that says CAUTION: PEOPLE. Maybe we would be a little more patient, a little more understanding, and a little friendlier to them. On any given day, "people" are dealing with something. They are stressed to the max, and in need of a little human kindness. This person's concerns are just as important to them as yours are to you. Someone's husband lost his job yesterday, someone learned that a nephew has cancer, and someone's daughter forgot to subtract the mortgage payment and is bouncing checks all over town. They may not be acting like it at the moment, but their time is valuable and their struggles are as real as yours. They are people, and need some space. CAUTION: PEOPLE might be a good reminder for all of us. If, however, I ever get behind a horse trailer with the warning CAUTION: HORSE DRIVING, I will think twice before I pass at all.

Jesus in a Bottle

The idea for this note started with an acquaintance of mine who is praying fervently for her boss to buy a coffee pot for the office. She's not praying for a generic pot; she's praying for a specific brand of coffee pot. She told me once that I needed to "ask the Lord" to speak to her boss concerning the purchase of this coffee pot.

As I thought about this, I recalled an incident from many years back, when a friend called to inform me that her husband had died that week. I expressed my sincere sympathy to her, and she said to me, "David, my husband is with the Lord." Now, I've heard that expression from people in bereavement hundreds of times, but I began to think about this particular phrase and did a little online research. I learned that, worldwide, there will be about 150,000 deaths every day. For the sake of discussion, let's say that the evangelicals are correct and that only 20 percent of those will get to heaven. That means that on any given day, about 30,000 people are now "with the Lord." Now, if they mean that the loved one is in heaven, and the Lord is in heaven, then I see how that would work. The feeling I get, however, is that the sentiment is that they are physically sitting there beside Jesus. Not only that, they are going to be "with the Lord" forever. Thirty thousand a day, every day, added to be "with the Lord." But if that provides comfort for you, I certainly wouldn't want to take that away. And, honestly, I say it quite often to bereaved people.

Along those lines, though, when my time comes and I get to heaven, I will ask to see my family, my clan, and a few of my closest friends. Then I want to talk to Albert Einstein. Of course, I would like to meet Jesus, but with as many people as he has to see, I can't imagine spending more than a few minutes with him. After all, thirty thousand people a day is a lot of traffic to manage. If one second of his voice lasted my whole life on earth, shouldn't 10 minutes with him last an eternity in heaven? I have a lot of questions for John about Chapter 1, verse 1. A lot of questions. And I have questions for the Apostle Paul, and what he had against women.

Recently, I talked with someone who referred to "the Lord" several times in every sentence of a speech he had given. In this case, he not only talked to the Lord, but apparently "the Lord" talked back to him regularly. Let me say at this point, I'm pretty sure that the Lord spoke to me once many years ago, but it was only once and only for a second. I will never forget the moment, and can take you to the exact spot where it happened. A second with the Lord was about all I could handle, but this speaker seemed to be able to rub the bottle, wait for Jesus to pop out, and grant him three (or more) wishes.

For the record, I maintain an active and ongoing relationship with Jesus, and believe that the Spirit of Christ resides in my heart and influences daily actions, thoughts, and words. I ask him often to guide my steps, to protect those that I love, and yes, I confess, I occasionally ask him to provide convenient parking spaces (but only when absolutely necessary!). I rarely expect him to answer me back, and truthfully don't expect him to provide the office with a coffee pot. After all, that's why he created Wal-Mart!

Losing my Voice, Finding my Center

Until recent years, I spent my whole life singing. I remember when I was a three-year-old, standing beside our record player, singing at the top of my lungs, "Home is where I hang my heart—so carry me back to that old Virginie shack, 'cause home is where I hang my heart." I sang in children's choirs, youth choirs, adult choirs, college choirs, and any choir that I could be a part of. I sang duets with my brother, solos every chance I got, and sang at my church, and churches across my community. I sang all the time. I became a voice major in college at Samford University in Birmingham, Alabama, and then continued vocal studies at the Southern Baptist Theological Seminary in Louisville, Kentucky. I sang leading roles in operas during my college years, and performed in opera choruses with the Louisville Opera Association, and later with the Chattanooga Symphony and Opera Association. For three incredible years, I sang and toured with the Samford University A Cappella Choir. During my graduate work in Louisville, I was selected to be a part of a 40-voice choir that performed Handel's *Messiah* with the Louisville Symphony, and was honored to be the bass soloist for an original work composed by my voice professor. After graduation, I routinely sang solos in my role as a minister of music for my church, and at community and civic events. My wife, an accomplished accompanist and vocalist in her own right, made it easy for me. Sharing music was extremely important for both of us, and something we loved doing. It was a touchstone in our marriage, and a part of our personal identities.

    The ability to take rumblings in my chest, resonate them in my head, and let them pour out of my mouth, is something only another singer can understand. Through singing, I expressed my deepest convictions, thoughts, and feelings. I often felt that, while singing, I was at my very best. Several years ago, however, I noticed when my range began to slip. Instead of being able to sustain an F, an E became the upper limit. When the E scooped down to E-flat, I noticed, and knew that something was physically different. I sought the advice of a medical doctor who scoped my throat and didn't find any structural problems. His advice was to just keep singing as well as I could. My range continued to slide, and soon I was having trouble sustaining lower notes. Singing became less fun, and more like work, and soon just felt impossible. The last solo that I performed was for a friend's funeral service a few years ago. The church was packed to capacity and I was mortified that I wouldn't make it to the end. I managed to finish the song without major humiliation and decided that day to hang up my spikes.

That was several years ago, and for a long time, the loss of my vocal ability seemed like a death in the family. Singing for so long had been my outward expression of so much of my life, and it left a huge void. Frankly, I also missed the applause and recognition that performing had brought through the years. It had felt really good to be really good, and to have people appreciate it so much. Sometime back, however, I realized that I had to give it up and move on. I wish I could tell you that I have replaced singing with something equally meaningful and personally fulfilling, but that would not be true. I can tell you, however, that I had to find another center, something deeper and more permanent than the ability to sing a solo. My personal circle of power has become: "Life is Good." That's it. Life is good. I have learned to appreciate that I am alive, and that the things that matter to me most are fully intact. I have gained much more than I lost. I have also learned to continue to express myself with words. Instead of having them come out of mouth in the form of notes and music, I have learned to let them come from inside me in the form of words and paragraphs on paper. I write often, and my writing has become my form of expression. For now, that is enough.

For the past six years, I have politely declined invitations to sing for weddings and funerals. Recently, my pastor asked me if I would sing for our church congregation at any time. Instead of saying no, I heard myself saying that I would consider it and let him know. My wife and I brushed up an old gospel favorite, "I've Never Been out of His Care," which I have sung dozens of times. It has a fairly narrow range, and for the most part, was still manageable. So I said yes, and I did it. Hopefully, I was the only one there who knew the extent of what I've lost. I'm quite certain that I'm the only one who knows how much I've gained.

A Light Unto My Path

When our only son was young, we frequently had need for a babysitter since we had no relatives living nearby. His favorite by far was a young lady named Stephanie. She was a young teenager who talked to him, played with him, and when she was old enough to drive, took him to fun destinations on their weekend visits. "Stephie" was queen.

At that time, Stephanie lived with her family in Chattanooga Valley, a small community at the foot of Lookout Mountain, Georgia. Before she had her driver's license, I would drive down to the valley to pick her up and then return her after our evening ended. One summer night on such a drive, I noticed a thunderstorm developing over the mountain, and decided to drive up to the top of the mountain to see the storm up close and personal. At that time, I was operating under the false information that car tires were an excellent insulation in the event of a lightning strike. (I have since learned, according to a Google search, that a typical bolt of lightning contains about a billion volts and 100,000 amps of electricity.) A friend of mine recently told me (after hearing my story), "If you think a half-inch of rubber is going to stop a bolt of lightning from getting to the ground, you should think again!" By the grace of God, I didn't get into weather trouble that night and lived to tell the tale.

This particular night was in the mid-1980s, and there were no CDs, no Apple music or SiriusXM, and the only music I had in the car that night was from a cassette tape. I was listening to one of my favorites at the time, from an Amy Grant album, "Straight Ahead." When I got to the top of the mountain, I parked my car, turned off the headlights, and waited. With no lights of any kind nearby, I waited in complete darkness. At first, the lightning was a good distance away, but within minutes it came closer and closer. Since I was "safe" in my car, I had no fear, and as the lightning began to pop all around me in a brilliant display, the tape cycled into another song on the same album, "Thy Word." Accompanied by constant claps of thunder and spectacular light, Amy Grant sang:

> Thy Word is a lamp unto my feet, and a light unto my path.
> Thy word is a lamp unto my feet and a light unto my path.
> When I feel afraid, and think I've lost my way—Still, you're right there beside me. Nothing will I fear as long as you are near; please be near me to the end.[1]

Now, instead of darkness, I was in light as bright as day. I could see the mountain and the valley for miles in the middle of the night. The flashes were blinding and the percussion was deafening. But I wasn't afraid; my tires were made of rubber. As the storm continued to move over my head and then off in the distance, the thunder changed to distant kettledrum beats instead of clashing cymbals. As a young boy, I had learned a verse in Vacation Bible School, Psalm 119:105, which talks about this lamp for my feet, and I had always pictured myself walking along a path with a flashlight or lantern. After that night, however, with the incredible symphony of sound and light that I had witnessed, the "light unto my path" was no less than the light of all the heavens illuminating the world around me.

Since then, when I think of that verse or hear that song, I am reminded that the light God shines on my path is not that of a lantern, but the light of the sun. The light that God shines is not just enough to keep me from stumbling in the dark, but is enough for me to see my way clearly. The path is not always easy, but at least I can see where I'm going.

Because of my Google search and the education of my well-informed friend, I have never put myself in harm's way again when it comes to thunderstorms, but because of my ignorance and the laws of nature, on that particular night, I had an unforgettable experience. The next time that you feel lost and afraid, imagine yourself surrounded by a billion volts of light, and in a protected cocoon of love and grace.

> "Nothing will I fear
> As long as you are near
> Please, be near me to the end."[2]

[1] Amy Grant, "Thy Word," 1983-1984, track 5 on *Straight Ahead*, Myrrh, 1984, album.

[2] Amy Grant, "Thy Word."

A Funny Story

Our refrigerator had been chirping for several days, and we finally decided that it wasn't going to stop on its own. Unless, of course, the whole thing just gave up the ghost. So, in order to avoid that outcome, we called a repairman. He suggested in our conversation that it might need a new motor and that he would come prepared to replace it.

When the serviceman arrived the next morning, we were engaging in casual small talk and he said, "I'm just waiting to hear the noise." Well, the refrigerator was chirping away as we talked, and I wasn't sure why he wasn't hearing it, but I suggested that he might take a look at our icemaker while we waited. For months, it had been delivering crushed ice instead of cubed ice—not a terrible problem, but while we waited, it gave us something to focus on.

I left him to work and went downstairs to read. After about half an hour, he called to me that he was finished, so I went up to pay and see him out. As I walked into the kitchen, the first sound I heard was the chirping of the refrigerator, and he was saying, "I never did hear your noise in the refrigerator," so I said, "Do you not hear it now?" He looked at me, smiled, and told me that I needed to check the battery in my smoke detector. I opened the cabinet door above the refrigerator, retrieved the chirping smoke alarm and removed the battery. The chirping stopped immediately. At least we got cubed ice out of the deal.

The Cost of Kindness

There is absolutely no cost of kindness. In every situation, in the same amount of time and with the same amount of effort that it takes to be short or rude, one can be kind. There are very few situations where kindness is not in order.

Just this morning, I was reminded of this fact. It was a small thing, and won't change my life either way, but it struck a nerve. I stopped at a convenience store to get gas and went in for a cup of coffee. I looked in the usual corners and didn't see the coffee stand; I could smell it, but I just didn't see it. Granted, a convenience store has a limited number of places to hide the coffee pot, but the clerk was standing right there in front of me, so I just asked her, "Would you mind pointing me to the coffee pot?" Without saying a word or even moving her head, she shifted her eyes to her left and maintained a countenance devoid of human compassion or feeling. I got the message, though. I looked over my shoulder at the coffee pot, which was, in fact, right behind me. I paid for my beverage, wished her a good day, and left.

Off and on today, I have thought about this encounter. How much effort would it have taken for her to smile and say, "Sir, it's right there behind you," or "If it were a snake, it would have bitten you!" She could have offered, "You're standing close enough to pour it already." Any number of friendly comments she could have made, but, instead, she said nothing and gave me the requested information with a stare that also said, "You're standing on it, you idiot, and furthermore you are wasting my precious time."

If my parents didn't teach me anything else, they taught me from the cradle to be kind and gracious toward people; people I know and people that I don't know. My dad drilled into my head in big and small ways that being kind and courteous isn't just next to godliness, it IS godliness.

They taught me to respect people and honor them as deserving of every effort with goodness and consideration.

"What the world needs now is love, sweet love" was important when the song was popular. And it still is. I can't think of a better time in the history of humanity when a little love and kindness is more needed, and would do more good for all of us. It's definitely time to stop and smell the coffee.

ANT Problems

For most of my life, I've been told that I think too much. I don't see that I have much choice where this is concerned, but I think too much. I'm nowhere near being on par with the genius, but just after Albert Einstein came out with E=MC2, I bet nobody said, "Albert, you think too much!"

I started thinking too much when I was a kid. When I was a ten-year-old, two rather traumatic things happened in and around my life, and I started thinking too much then. I can remember as a sixth grader when my teacher, Mr. Di Michelle, told us that the sun was going to burn out eventually. It didn't matter to me that this event would be billions of years away; it just mattered that the center of our solar system would someday die. So I thought about that. A lot. I still think about it.

Thinking too much, in and of itself, is not necessarily a bad thing. It's the things we choose to think too much about that can get bad for us. Most of the time, when we see, hear, think, or feel something, another something gets triggered; that "something else" is often bad, sad, or otherwise uncomfortable. It's unfortunate that many of us are wired that way. This can often mean that if we leave our mental processes to themselves, we are much of the time distressed. I recently took one of the standardized "100 point stress tests" and landed exactly where I expected—right in the high stress category. I was given a little stress ring, but I gave it to my granddaughter. She likes jewelry. And she thinks too much, too.

One of my favorite stress relievers is to wander around Barnes and Noble bookstore from time to time and just peruse their shelves. I wander around until I find something that looks interesting, take it with me to the Starbucks (in the bookstore), get a cup of coffee, find somewhere to sit, and just read and enjoy my coffee. Sometimes, I actually buy the book, but not usually. Recently, in the self-help section, I found a book on thinking that caught my eye. Looking through the table of contents, I saw a chapter on ANTS—Automatic Negative Thinking. I knew without reading it that I could have written that chapter. As I suspected, the chapter was on the process of attaching negative thoughts to other thoughts. The phenomenon happens because the chemicals and wiring in our brains are all connected. The things we see, think, and feel, are attached to other parts of our brains. Thought A triggers memories B, C, and D. These memories can be as recent as 10 minutes ago, or 45 years ago. The brain also makes no distinction of time. Those memories from 45 years ago can be as powerful as when the event occurred. If you have accumulated ANTs from all of last week, you have a problem. If you've been accumulating them from a lifetime, then you have a serious problem.

The only way to deal with ANTs is to learn to let them go and replace them with positive memories. The Zen folks tell us that, in order to deal with distracting thoughts during meditation, you see it, look at it, and let it go. This is much easier said than done, but it is possible, even for an over-thinker like me. Years ago, I read an interesting illustration about this that likened our thoughts to placing a needle on a record album. Once the needle finds a particular groove, it plays the same song over and over. For that matter, it will play it in exactly the same way. The only way to overcome ANTs is to create new grooves in the recording. It's not enough to say, "I'm not going to continue to dwell on this negative stuff." You have to create new associations.

Jon Katob-Zinn is a world-renowned expert on mindfulness meditation. He says that the key to successful meditation, and thus the key to positive thinking habits, is to "be here, now." Be here—not somewhere else—but here. Be now. Be "alive in the present moment."

So the next time ANTs are crowding your mental space, just think about something good in that situation. You can always find something good about it if you try. See it, look at it, and let it go. If the problem persists, consider calling an exterminator.

Bibliomancy: Remembering the Eagles

In the fall of 1972, I applied to be a summer missionary through the Home Mission Board of the Southern Baptist Convention. After a few weeks, I received a letter telling me that I had been accepted into the program, and that I would be spending my summer in Eatontown, New Jersey. I was excited already. That spring, I got a letter from the board telling me that I would need to attend an orientation at Shocco Springs, the Baptist Assembly in Talladega, Alabama. I would be there with many other students who would also be spending their summers as missionaries all over the United States. This assembly was a special place for me already, as I had gone there for various church camps in my childhood, and had already had several profound encounters with God (or Somebody important) over the years. I was looking forward to this trip on so many levels, among them the chance to get away from home, school, family, and friends for a few days. I felt that I needed to get my head together a bit. WWJD (and trying to live exactly by that rule) was making me very tired, and I just needed a break.

When I arrived at camp on Friday afternoon, I was given the weekend schedule, and quickly found a two-hour block of free time on Saturday afternoon. I knew that was going to be my time to get away to the nearby mountains to let my soul catch up with my body. The student worship service on Friday night was very meaningful, and I was feeling "connected"—feeling that Something greater was happening for me—yet I still looked forward to Saturday afternoon and free time.

After lunch, someone stood to make an announcement. "A meeting has been added to the schedule for those of you who will be summer missionaries. It will be held at 2 p.m., and is a very important meeting that all are required to attend." I was deflated. I couldn't believe that my retreat had been taken away. At this point in the story, you need to understand a little bit about me. I was a rules kind of guy. My father was extremely strict about OBEYING THE RULES. He taught us the importance of living up to the expectations of people around us (something I still struggle with). In other words, if I was expected to attend the meeting, then other options weren't available to me. Walking back to my dorm after lunch, though, I made an important and grown-up decision. As important as this meeting surely was, my free time was even more important on this particular day. I decided that I would find out what I had missed after the fact. I even allowed myself the potential to disappoint my roommate and others in the program. So with my Bible in hand and hope in my heart, I headed out.

I found a path that day which was new to me. I wandered the path into a wooded area and up into the hills. After I had walked for about 30 minutes or so, I settled down on a hillside overlooking a valley below. It was a beautiful spring day of sunshine, beautiful and clear. Birds were singing, flowers were blooming, and it was a perfect day. In the midst of all that, however, there was the nagging thought about what I was missing and the people I was disappointing back down at the camp. I managed to push it aside and enjoy the serenity around me. Until that moment, I hadn't noticed the eagle's nest in a tree about 20 feet below me. I looked up as the mother bird soared above me, making gentle circles, climbing, falling, gliding, and flying all around me. I was transfixed—spellbound. This was my first experience with an eagle in such an up close and personal way. Well-meaning people later suggested that I witnessed a hawk in flight, but I knew the difference. It was an eagle. As I watched, the bird's circles got smaller and it came closer and closer to where I was sitting, landing in her nest just below me. She brought food to her waiting babies, and I watched them eagerly accept her offering. They sang and chirped. After a while, she spread her wings, caught a breeze, and was again lifted from the nest and made lazy circles above me. The thought occurred to me that these birds were enjoying life much more than I was! I decided that I wanted to find a way to enjoy life, and to be the person that I was created to be. I sat in silence for a long time, trying to understand the meaning of what was happening in front of my eyes. I prayed for quite some time and asked God to help me give up my rigid thinking, to be open to the ease of beauty and truth, the truth that sets us free.

I had intended to spend time that afternoon reading my Bible, but "the Word" had other ideas about how to spend my time. As important as daily Bible study was to me at that time, the "day with the eagles" on that beautiful spring day was much more significant.

When the time came for me to go back to the camp, I began to think about the consequences that I would have to face for "breaking the rules" and missing the meeting. I breathed a prayer, "God, I feel in my soul that this encounter with you was much more important than a meeting. I don't have the heart to feel bad about it, but I would like to open my Bible to a verse about David, or maybe a mountain. If you will do that for me, I won't give it another thought. Either way, thank you for this incredible time with you today. Amen." I opened my Bible and, with the living God as my witness, put my finger on the page and read: "Saul and his men were on one side of the mountain and David and his men were on the other side" (1 Samuel 23:26).

I don't remember my walk back to the camp, but I imagine that I flew back, much like the eagle. Neither do I remember what I missed that afternoon at the meeting. I do remember, though, that this particular afternoon was the beginning of a healing in my mind and spirit that continues to this day. My dear dad is long gone, but rules still give me pause.

Star Stuff

"In thee, O Lord, do I put my trust...for Thou art my rock and my fortress" Psalm 31:1, 3 (KJV).

We are all made of star stuff. That's not an original with me; I'm quoting Carl Sagan, from a television special that I saw many years ago. But just this past Sunday evening, I heard it again, this time from a scientist on a show I caught on the History Channel.

I am absolutely intrigued with this universe we live in, and have been since my sixth grade science class with Mr. Di Michelle. One morning, Mr. D. told us something that bothered me a lot. He was discussing the sun, and how its internal fusion continues to create its own energy. He explained that this energy is transferred to us some 93 million miles away. The light from the sun travels at 186,000 miles per second, but even at that speed, it takes eight minutes for the heat and light to reach us. I was doing fine with all this information until he said, "But one day it will burn out." Granted, he went on to say that this would be billions and billions of years from now, several years past my lifetime, but that part didn't matter. It stopped me cold in my tracks that it would burn out. It bothered me. It was the first time I was aware of my own mortality. I knew that if the sun died, then I would die. We would all die.

Even with that disturbing start, I became increasingly fascinated with the heavens around us. At this point, you would expect to hear about my first telescope or my recent trip to an observatory, but no. I have spent my life reading and thinking about it all. There have been wonderful moments of connection, of course; there was the night when I was perched at the edge of the Grand Canyon and watched the Hale-Bopp Comet suspended in space above my head. But for the most part, I'm a reader, and occasional observer of science broadcasts.

Scientists estimate that our medium-sized galaxy, the Milky Way, is about 100,000 light years across, and contains about 100 million suns. That's a fairly large area. These same scientists also postulate that there are billions of galaxies in our known universe. With the immensity of those numbers, the part of the broadcast that intrigues me most is the part where they talk about the basic elements of which it's all made. It is conjectured—well, fairly accurately calculated—that there were only two elements created in the first seconds of the Big Bang: hydrogen and helium. That's it. Two elements. Everything else was synthesized in the heart of all those stars. Over billions of years, that stuff, all those other elements, found its way to our lonely planet and, a few billion years later, life was created. We are indeed star stuff. The narrator said, "We are a part of the universe and it is a part of us." So tonight, when you look up into the sky at your favorite constellation, consider the fact that it's your mother, your father, you. We came from there.

So, just because scientists, based on empirical and hypothetical data, think all of this is true, does it mean that it all happened this way? Well, no. But isn't it fun to think that when you wish upon a star, no matter who you are, the star has at least a tiny memory of you? Wishes just got a lot better!

The Gospel According to Waffle House

For those of you who do not live in the southeastern United States, Waffle House is a restaurant. There are 1,500 of them in 25 states and while most of them are along interstate highways, many of them are not. Whoever said, "The whole is greater than the sum of its parts," and whatever they said it about, could definitely have been phrased with Waffle House in mind. The food is good—not great—well, except for their breakfast food. Until recently, their small "no smoking" section was like having a "no peeing" section in a public swimming pool. However, thanks to smoking bans everywhere, Waffle House restaurants are now smoke free (and if they weren't, I wouldn't be there). Generally, you will find Waffle House to be a relatively small restaurant, and they're all built exactly the same. They are rectangular box buildings with a big yellow and black Waffle House sign spelled out in yellow and black Scrabble-like lettering. It's as recognizable as the golden arches. When you walk inside, there are about eight booths for a party of four and maybe ten or twelve stools at an L-shaped counter. They request that you reserve the booths for parties of two or more, but they have never pressed the issue, and they let you sit where you sit. I generally respect their request when dining alone. The grill is right in the center of the room so that the aroma of the food being prepared fills the whole room. The waitresses and waiters have shelves below the counter and out of sight, and keep the dishes washed and ready at all times, almost as if by magic. The prices are also reasonable when you pay attention to the menu offerings and to what you're doing. This morning I had a breakfast of two eggs, soft scrambled, two slices of wheat toast, hash browns, and coffee for less than five dollars!

    The thing that came to me recently in the middle of the night, though, is that Waffle House is a little like God, or vice versa. All 1,500 of the stores are open seven days a week, 24 hours a day, no exceptions. The night I had my revelation around 2 a.m., it occurred to me that I could get up, get dressed, get into my car, and drive 15 minutes in just about any direction, and arrive at any of six Waffle House restaurants! Now not everybody is blessed with so many choices, and it's not all that unusual to stop at an interstate Waffle House and look across the highway to see one on the other side. They are ubiquitous!

So, on the night of my inspiration, I thought, "You know, I don't really want to get up, get dressed, get into my car, and drive to a Waffle House, but I really like knowing that they are all there." I like knowing that if I did all of the above, that whichever one I chose, when I walked in the door at whatever time of day or night, I would be greeted with "Welcome to Waffle House! Take a seat anywhere you'd like!" The servers, for the most part, are friendly and courteous, and will immediately pour you a cup of steaming hot coffee, and are ready to take your order as soon as you're ready. Then there's the cook. I have learned that there is a "system," but I'm fairly amazed at how they work. The servers shout orders to him (seems that it's usually a "him," but not necessarily) from all sides, almost all at once. He is pulling pans from left and right and cracking eggs, frying sausage and bacon, while putting mayo on bread for a BLT. Meanwhile, the wait staff is still barking orders. Very seldom have I seen a cook appear to be flustered or confused. After watching the routine, one night I just had to ask how the cook was able to keep all the orders straight. My server asked me, "Do you see those plates with jelly on the edges? Well, the way those jellies are placed on the plate is how the cook keeps up with the orders." I replied "Ohhhhh!" But like I say, I'm impressed.

Then there's the Waffle House music. I am not a big fan of country music, but what would Waffle House be without it? It is just part of the fabric, much like the big yellow sign, the waitresses, the coffee, and the cook.

My point? I'm not sure yet. But it's something like this: as with God, they are always open for business, and also like Him, much of it is still a great mystery. But it's comforting to know that no matter where I go, and what time of day or night, I can pull off the highway where I see the bright yellow sign. I can park my car, walk in the door, and receive a friendly welcome and a good cup of coffee, and rest along my journey. Thank God for Waffle House!

But Don't Forget Your Bucket!

My inspiration for these thoughts came while reading *Sacred Spaces: Stations on a Celtic Way*, by Margaret Silf, while sitting on the deck of a beach house in Laguna Beach, Florida. My backdrop was the sand and surf of the Gulf of Mexico, and my then three-month-old granddaughter was asleep in the next room. It wasn't difficult to find inspiration under these circumstances.

But I'm back home now—no sand, no surf, no seagulls, or pelicans. And my granddaughter has gone home as well. My backdrop is the sound of the washing machine and dishwasher cleaning their respective loads, performing their prescribed tasks.

As many times as I've heard or read the story of "the woman at the well," what I'm writing now had never occurred to me until I was reading the story again this week. Besides her artful descriptions of seven stations, or sacraments, of the "Celtic way," Silf includes several poetic paraphrases of well-known Bible stories in her book, including that of John 4, the wonderful and warm-hearted story of Jesus' chance encounter with this Samaritan woman.

There is so much to the story, and so many different angles from which to approach it, that I find it difficult to narrow my focus to the point that I actually want to make. So, I'll just get to the point and go from there. The point is this: Whatever Jesus meant when he told the Samaritan woman that he was going to give living water, he didn't mean that she would, nor would those who depended on her, never again need to draw the water. When she left the well that day to go back into the city to tell her friends about this remarkable man who told her everything she had done, she should not have left her bucket. Before the day was over, or certainly by the next day, she was going to need it again.

Besides the narrative including Jesus and the Samaritan woman and the perplexed disciples, there is the underlying story of the water in Jacob's well versus the "living water" that only Jesus can provide. All of us are thirsty. We were born and remain thirsty for all of our lives. Experts tell us that we can live for weeks without food, but will survive only a matter of days without water. People deprived of water do desperate things to survive. Whatever Jesus meant when he told the woman about the "living water," he didn't mean that she would never experience physical thirst again. He said that it would become "a well of water springing up to eternal life." She's the one who suggested that with this water she would never again be thirsty and never again have to draw water from Jacob's well.

Granted, this woman, like all of us, had needs that far transcended what a bucket of water could meet. Whatever else she needed, she needed to be loved and accepted by a man; she had already had five husbands, and her current partner was not her husband. She needed to feel attractive, to be needed as a person and not just for the pleasure she could give to a man. This water in the well could not touch that. Only Jesus could help fulfill that need, and he did. She was sick and tired of making this same hot, dusty, lonely trek day after empty day, and pulling water up some 250 feet, only to lug it back home to a man who didn't appreciate her or the water that she brought to him. Then she experienced Jesus. She received love from a man who only wanted to help her find the wellspring within herself that could provide the love and grace that she so desperately needed. That's what we all seek. The story leads us to believe that she found what she had been looking for.

But she shouldn't have left her bucket. Before the day was over, she would be thirsty, and her family would need water. Herein lies the great paradox of living. While we are all starving for the abundant life that only Jesus can provide, our bodies are constantly starving for the daily rations of basic sustenance. But once those basic necessities are met, we still feel empty and are left asking, "Is that all?" I want more. I need more. I read the Bible, go to church, pray daily, and yet I am starving for a drink of the living water of Jesus. Where can I find it? Where can I drink it? Is this all there is to the Living Way of Jesus? The last time I saw Maslow's hierarchy of needs, it occurred to me that we don't climb that pyramid for a lifetime and finally reach the eternal bliss of self-actualization; we climb up and down that pyramid of needs several times a day. You may be in a state of enlightenment, but when your stomach growls, you're right back down at the food, clothing, and shelter level again.

The answer that Jesus gave is that this "well of water springing up to eternal life" is already within each of us. You don't need a bucket. You don't have to go to the beach to find it. You don't have to read a devotional book, and you certainly won't find it by abusing alcohol or drugs. Jesus said, "The kingdom of God is within you." Stop trying to find it. If you have the love and light of Jesus in you, then you already have it. Silf continues in her writing, "If you could, you would know yourself, and you would know and recognize the real me—you would find a well of life itself in my heart, and in your own."

But don't forget your bucket. Before the day is over, you're going to need it. If you are ever to experience the kingdom of God within you, you're going to have to find it while going about your daily life. It's when you're able to make that long, dusty, lonely walk to the well, knowing God's presence along the way that His living water bubbles up to eternal life. God create us all as needy human beings. Frederick Buechner said, "Man does not live by bread alone, but he can't live all that long without it, either."[1]

I must admit, after the dishwasher stopped, I inserted my favorite CD into the computer, *The Complete A Cappella Works of Eric Whitacre*, and continued to write (working in the kitchen, by the way, as my office has temporarily been converted into a nursery). The story doesn't tell us, but I feel quite certain that the first thing Jesus did after the woman left for town was to use her bucket to get some water. He more than likely asked one of the disciples to share a sandwich, too.

"Believe me, the time will come when we will all come to realize that the whole of creation is sacred ground—wells and churches and cathedrals, no less, no more than your own back yard. I know that one day these things will be true, perhaps in heaven. Jesus told her 'heaven is here and now.' The secret is in your heart and your own life, only waiting to open up and grow into fullness."[2]

It's easy for us to experience the presence of God while sitting with our feet propped up, overlooking the Gulf of Mexico, or listening to our favorite music, but like Br. Andrew, it's only when we experience him in our hearts while clearing the table and washing dishes that the kingdom is near.

[1] Frederick Buechner, *The Alphabet of Grace* (New York: Harper and Row, 1970.)

[2] Margaret Silf, *Sacred Spaces: Stations on a Celtic Way*. (Massuchusetts: Paraclete Press, 2001.)

Remembering Maggie

December 14, 1994–March 13, 2008

When my son was 13 years old, he announced (over and over again) that he wanted a puppy. Frankly, so did I. Okay, maybe it was the other way around. I really wanted a dog, and what better way to disguise that than to cloak it in the wishes of a child? Anyway, two out of three in the household wanted a dog, and even in Congress that's enough to override a veto!

My wife gave the two of us advanced directives. First, the dog will live outside; build him a fence/pen first. Secondly, this will be YOUR dog! So my brother-in-law and I took his truck to Lowe's department store and bought all we needed to erect a fenced-in area for our dog. I worked for an entire day building the pen, constructing it out of top posts, side posts, fencing, and concrete. I used a come-along fastened to trees to pull the wire tight on all sides and it was a masterpiece. At the end of the day, I was proud of my handiwork. We would later know that the pen would rarely keep the dog inside it. I used extra wire, wooden blocks, chains on the door, extra concrete, and Maggie was always able to find a way out. The first day we had her, we were eating dinner when our neighbor rang the doorbell with our puppy in her hands and said, "I think this is your dog."

The day we went to the Chattanooga Humane Society, I had sat for a grueling exam in preparation for the Certified Financial Planner designation. I was mentally exhausted, but this was the day we had set aside to get a puppy, so we were both excited. The stench at the Humane Society that day was particularly bad, almost overpowering. We pressed along, however, moving from cage to cage, viewing the puppies that were available. Dave had been saying for weeks, "I don't want no girl dog," and I assured him that a boy dog would be just fine. We looked into one of the little cages, and huddled together like two peas in a pod, were two little balls of black fur. At first glance, it looked like one shaggy puppy, but two definite little bodies were sleeping side by side. My little boy picked up both of them, cuddled them, and looked them over really well. They were beautiful little black and brown puppies with white paws, one male and the other female. Besides her beautiful coat, the female had one sky blue eye and the other eye was half blue and half brown. He said, "I want her."

I paid $25, signed some papers saying that we would love her and if we ever decided not to love her, that we would bring her back to them. Officially, the papers said "mixed shepherd," and we had no idea what she would grow up to be. That $25 turned out to be one of the most expensive purchases I have ever made, but it was also one of the best investments of my life.

When we got home with our little ball of fur, because she still smelled like a sewer, we bathed her—twice—and let her take a nap on our bed, because Mom was at work and nobody said we couldn't. We did take a picture, though, which my wife found sometime later. How smart was that?

Maggie quickly became one of us. We tease about her being basically worthless. She was never one for fetching sticks and balls. She never learned to roll over or chase her tail. She never brought me the daily paper or slippers, and she never pulled anyone from a burning building. She just was. She loved us and she let us love her. We fed her and bathed her. We scratched her head and rubbed her belly. Maggie was not much for kissing, and rarely licked our faces, but occasionally, after I had given her particular attention, she would lick my hand to say "Thanks. That felt good. I love you, too."

But she did play "sheet." Sheet was exactly that. She created the game herself when we would pull out an old sheet that we used for hauling off leaves after raking the yard. One day, she pounced on the sheet, grabbed a corner and took off. The game involved rolling her up in the sheet and making her find her way out. A passerby might have thought it cruel because she would get so wound up trying to escape, but she loved it. She would grab onto one corner and wait for me to grab another, and a ferocious game of tug of war would ensue. Maggie always outlasted me, so I guess, technically, she always won. We played many hours of sheet, and took way too long getting the yard work done. Even when she was so sick, we played sheet to the end.

Maggie was funny in a Helms sort of way. None of us are that much at telling funny stories, but all of us like to tease and create "situation humor." Maggie was no different. To the delight of friends and guests who happened to be watching, Maggie would scratch her own back by sliding down the hill in our front yard. She accomplished this feat by walking to the top of the hill, rolling on her back, extending all fours skyward, and wrenching back and forth as she slid down the hill while maintaining her position and balance, groaning in ecstasy the whole way down. One afternoon, I watched one of my son's friends observing this. He didn't say a word until Maggie was at the bottom of the hill and then remarked, "I think that's the most amazing thing I've ever seen."

Like most dogs, Maggie loved to be loved. Anytime I would sit on the front porch, she would come running; tail wagging, with her eyes on fire. She would climb up the steps, come around from behind, stick her snout under my arm, and with a jerk of her head, toss my limp arm into the air so that she would slip beside me and have my arm fall on her head. Granted, I could have just scratched her head, but I enjoyed the routine. Maggie was not the brightest star in the sky, but she wasn't dumb either. The only time she was really a nuisance surrounded her habit of chewing the woodwork around our front door. We were never able to figure out what caused this behavior, and the vet didn't have any answers for us. She suggested that it might be boredom, or something missing from her diet, or perhaps "getting even" for being left alone longer than she liked. We decided that she just liked to chew wood and gave her the nickname "Termite." In any case, we spent several hundred dollars having the woodwork replaced—twice. We tried any number of ways to train her to stay off the steps. Surely you really can teach an old dog new tricks. Anytime I found her there chewing on the wood, I would swat her across the rump with a rolled up newspaper and yell, "Maggie! NO!" So when we were at home, for the most part, she stayed off the porch. After we had been gone awhile and would pull into the driveway, there we would find her, perched on the porch. By the time we could park the car and walk upstairs to open the door, she would be off the porch on the sidewalk just as she'd been trained to do. Good dog.

For the record, my wife loved Maggie as much as any of us did. She wouldn't openly admit it, because after all, this was MY DOG! But she's a softie and she grew to love Maggie just the same. Maggie had developed anxiety, and didn't do well in thunderstorms. There was a day when I came home on a bad weather day in a terrific downpour, parked my car, and was headed into the house when I heard my wife yelling for me. She was down at Maggie's pen on her knees, mired in mud, crying and begging for help. In her frightened effort to escape her fence, Mag had become stuck between the door and one of the poles. She was halfway in, halfway out, and her weight made it impossible to open the chain on the door to free her. Maggie was in a panic, her breathing shallow and frantic, and we both were afraid that we weren't going to be able to free her before she suffocated. I finally was able to put my knee into her side and loosen the chain to set her free. That's the last day she spent there. After that, we left the door open and she was free to be in and out as she chose. She never strayed, and by good luck we were able to avoid having her picked up in violation of our county leash laws. For her last years, she lived in and around the house, her spot in the front bushes well worn and burrowed. Our neighborhood had grown to love Maggie, so it wasn't a serious concern. (Well, most of the neighborhood, and in the end even he came around. I once saw the Grinch neighbor patting my dog's head.)

Maggie began to have "ailments"—after all, she was getting to be an old woman, and age shows itself. I took her to the vet in June with a very red and swollen eye. After being treated for eye infection without responding, our doctor referred us to a veterinary ophthalmologist.

He examined her thoroughly and told us that the news that day would not be good. Her problem was not with the eye, but with a tumor behind the eye causing the swelling and inflammation. We went back to our family veterinarian for a treatment protocol. The vet basically gave us the option to treat Maggie with what would be a long, painful, invasive, very expensive regimen, or to give her a few good weeks, and let her go.

The good weeks turned into good months. With good care and positive response to medication, Maggie lived with her tumor fairly comfortably for about four months when her quality of life showed signs of decline. All three of our animal doctors had given us "the talk" over the months and just before Christmas, while our son was home, we took Maggie to the clinic assuming that this would be our last visit. We were surprised with the news that, once again, an antibiotic and steroid might help her to rally. She responded well for another couple of weeks, but her health and general disposition began to decline rapidly. She had lost significant weight and had become weak and somewhat lifeless. The tumor in her brain had begun to grow into her mouth and was making her uncomfortable. She wasn't able to eat well, and when she began to develop a bed sore, it was decided that we had done all that could be done, and it was time to let her go.

On the ride to the clinic that afternoon, I scratched her head most of the way and reflected on our years together. How is it possible to love an animal so much? How is it possible that Maggie is about to NOT be? Right now, she's with me, but I'll be going home without her.

"Mr. Helms, Dr. Shaffeld is ready for you." I took Maggie into the treatment room where we had spent many hours over the years, especially in the last six months, and helped her onto the table. I stroked her fur and talked to her until the doctor was in the room. He explained to me what he was going to do, and let me know that within seconds after the injection, Maggie would be gone. He asked with compassion, "Are you ready for this?" Well, no. I had never experienced this before. My dog trusts me and loves me. Right now, she's still breathing and I'm giving this man permission to take that away. My friend Maggie is still alive. Twenty-five dollars. Thirteen years. Thirteen years with this beautiful, wood-chewing mutt. But, yes, I was ready. I kissed her on the head and said, "I love you, Maggie, and I'm sorry." He shaved a small patch of fur from her leg and gently pushed the needle into her vein. My sweet Maggie struggled for a few seconds, and then she died. He said that I could stay as long as I wanted, so I stayed a bit, covered her with a towel, and I left.

For the past two mornings, we have been greeted in the early hours by the sound of rolling thunder. I have found comfort in the fact that none of it was bothering Maggie at all. Is it possible that I sense her presence in the thunder, in the rain? For the rest of my life, thunder will be my cloud by day and my pillar by night in remembering the love and life of my dog, Maggie. Do all dogs really go to heaven? I don't know, but I'm pretty sure this one did.

Finding Inner Joy

I think about and write about happiness and joy because neither one comes naturally for me. I have to work at it. My default emotions involve stress, worry, and anxiety. So what I'm proposing for you to consider are things that I consider every day of my life. I've learned that no matter what I grew up with, I am responsible for my own feelings. My feelings are nobody's fault but mine.

These thoughts and suggestions will not help very much if your bad feelings are biochemical in nature. Biochemical problems demand biochemical solutions. Just as there are hundreds of medicines for physical ailments; there are also many medicines for mental issues. These suggestions are for garden-variety neurotics.

If you are postponing inner joy until your relationships with your parents are resolved, you will wait a long time. If you are procrastinating inner joy until you resolve your emotions left from childhood, then joy won't happen. If you're waiting for your financial situation to improve, you will have to wait months or years. You don't have to "find" inner joy; it's already in you. It's something you only have to remember. No matter how deprived and abused you may have been in the past or how deprived you are in the present, joy is still available. It is vitally important that you learn to feel good again. Joy is not a destination; it's the journey. There are hundreds of stories in scripture and in modern experience of people held captive or even tortured, who in the worst of circumstances experience something wonderful that springs from within them. I have read of Holocaust survivors, such as Victor Frankl, who describe this experience. The lesson is if you can fog a mirror you can experience joy.

Here's the problem with waiting for the reconciliation of past experiences, the termination of certain undesirable circumstances, or overcoming the fear of possible future outcomes before you allow yourself to feel good. When all of that has been resolved, there will always be something else bothering you, nagging at you. Joy is not something you can find. It's a gift; it can only be accepted.

Here are a few suggestions for finding inner joy right now in your current circumstances:

1. Find at least a few minutes each day to be still and quiet. Even if you never meditate for hours a day, just allow your soul to catch up with your mind and body. It's your personal time out. You make your children sit down, and then you sit down.
2. Learn to accept things the way they are. "It is what it is," as they say.
    a. Understand "what is" is not in your control (most things are not).
    b. As things invade your psyche, either act on them or let them go.
3. Finally, practice gratitude. The absolute shortest path to inner joy is to feel and express gratitude for all that you already have to enjoy. Say "thank you." "Thank you" releases powerful opiates that are hard-wired into your nervous system. It's healthy, it's free, and there are no harmful side effects.

When I was a child, we usually traveled U.S. 79 to Laguna Beach from Enterprise, Alabama. However, sometimes we would take a detour to a place called Flowing Wells. Flowing Wells was a spring behind a church that was piped up through a stone enclosure. There was magic when drinking that water from that fresh spring. It was a type of communion, if you please. We didn't have to turn on a faucet; we didn't need a glass or a container. All we had to do was bend over and drink the cold, clear water. I would like to suggest that experiencing inner joy is just like that. Jesus told the woman at the well that he would give her living water—that it was within her. As soon as she understood that, she ran to town, telling everyone that a man showed her where to find living water. That's the water I'm talking about. That's the joy I'm referring to. You will never "find joy" anywhere, but you can accept it. It's already yours.

Tombstone Territory

The only jury I have ever sat on was a very sad case. I have reported for jury duty a number of times, but this was the only time I was selected. The trial was at the Walker County Courthouse in Lafayette, Georgia (think luh FAY ette). The trial of Jones vs. Anderson was sister vs. sister—half-sisters to be exact. The family owned a cemetery plot in town where Jones' mother and father were buried. The plot had a single headstone with both of their names. When Anderson's father died, he was buried in the same plot and she wanted to erect a headstone for him. Jones said it would make the plot "uneven." Anderson erected a headstone anyway. A few days later, in the middle of the night, Jones and her husband used a pick and shovel to dig it up, cart the headstone off in a wheelbarrow, and dump it behind a shed. Then Jones sued her sister for damages to the gravesite. And there we were in court.

The trial lasted several days with brothers, sisters, aunts, uncles, neighbors, and friends all getting involved in the drama. Several members of the family expressed their extreme discomfort in having to take sides in the matter. Once a brother testifying for Jones looked down at Anderson from the witness stand and apologized for what he was doing. It was pitiful. Literally.

I had been elected foreman of the jury. I think it was because I was the only one wearing a tie the day we voted. So the members of the jury kept looking to me for guidance on what to do. We all wanted to rule in favor of Anderson, but we were hung up on one technicality. What sort of ownership did Anderson have in the plot? Did she have the legal right to erect that headstone? That fact had never come out during the proceedings. In Georgia, a foreman can't ask the judge a question in or out of the courtroom. I explained our dilemma to the bailiff and he explained it to the judge. I guess we made Georgia legal history. The judge had all the jurors file into the jury box. He looked at me and sternly asked, "What is your question?" And I told him. He then "read me my rights." "You are to reach a verdict based on what you have heard in this courtroom. The only evidence you can use to reach your decision is what you have heard in here." And then with a more stern expression, "Do you understand what I am telling you?" "Yes, your honor. I understand." We filed out of the courtroom and back into the deliberation room. After the firm reprimand, we knew what we had to do. If Anderson had never owned any part of the cemetery plot, she did now. Within minutes, we decided for Anderson and against Jones. We again filed into the courtroom. "All rise," etc. I handed our verdict to the bailiff and he handed it to the judge. "In the matter of Jones vs. Anderson, the court rules in favor of Anderson." And he pounded his gavel on the desk as he proclaimed, "Court dismissed." Anderson now did not have to pay any damages and she was free to put her father's headstone back on the plot. I hope that Jones and her husband had to do it.

The saddest part of the trial was not that it was sister vs. sister. Families do, in fact, feud. Families are not exempt from misunderstandings, deep divisions, and hard feelings toward each other. The saddest part to me is that Jones wanted to deprive her sister from honoring her father because it wouldn't look right. Looks do matter. Appearances are important. But there are times when it is appropriate and even necessary to choose function over form. There is a powerful scene in the movie *Ordinary People* that illustrates my point very well. The movie opens with the survival of a young man, Conrad, who attempted suicide after his older brother, Bucky, had died in a boating accident. Both of them were on that boat. The father, Cal, is trying to deal with his grief and with Conrad's pain and embarrassment. The mother, Beth, is trying to act like nothing happened. It's business as usual for her. Conrad and his father grow progressively closer, as Beth withdraws to a world of her own making. Toward the end of the movie, Cal asks Beth, "When we were getting ready for Bucky's funeral, you told me to wear my blue shirt." Beth turns to him absolutely stunned and asks, "What?" He repeats the statement and asks, "What difference did it make what shirt I wore to my son's funeral?" The next morning, she packs and leaves.

Did it really matter if the grave plot was a little "unbalanced"? Was it going to fall over? Was it going to be written up in the Lafayette society paper? The family could have discussed their differences over coffee and cake. Instead, lawyers, a judge, and jurors who gave of their time had to publically hash it out and tell them what to do. A few months later, I was in McDonald's in Ft. Oglethorpe, Georgia. While I was waiting my turn in line, I saw Jones across the restaurant. I thought, "What the heck?" and I looked her way and nodded. She walked over and asked, "I know you, don't I?" I responded, "Yes ma'am, I believe you do." She paused for a few seconds, smiled, and said, "I thought so."

Don't look up Jones vs. Anderson in the Walker County archives. Those are not their names. It doesn't matter. I keep intending to find that headstone and see our handiwork, but I just never have. "Let the dead bury their dead," Jesus said. And I'm quite sure he thought, "And let their families honor their remains."

Emotional Resources

July 4, 2019

My counselor and I are working on this idea of "emotional resources." In a few words, he said, "David, we all have a limited amount of emotional resources. We all have to decide how to spend them." I am finding that to be a very powerful statement. As an example, for years my extended family converged on the family beach house at Laguna Beach, Florida, for the fourth of July weekend. The group included my grandmother, her sister, my aunts and uncles, my mother and father, my siblings, my cousins, my wife, our son, and his cousins. There were about 25 of us in all. Besides spending time in the "cottage" (slept all 25 people), we also played on the beach. My uncle always brought a boat and we went water skiing at Phillips Inlet, about eight miles from the house. I had learned to ski and even to slalom at an early age and was really good on that ski. It was great fun for all of us. I had a reputation for being able to all but fall in the water, regain my balance, and keep skiing (they say it's not bragging if you did it).

So what does remembering this family gathering have to do with "emotional resources"? It has everything to do with them. This morning as I remembered those gatherings for over 30 years, I felt a wave of sadness. All but one uncle of that generation above me died several years ago. I have lost touch with most of those cousins. Well, really, all but one of them. My sister, brother, and I live in adjoining states and I only see them every now and then. The beach house was sold to a stranger years ago. I don't know who owns it now. So adding all that up, for a few minutes, I felt pretty crummy about all of that. Then I heard my counselor say, "You have to decide how you spend your limited emotional resources." In this case, I decided not to spend them in sadness over what was such a fabulous family tradition. In spite of the losses, I chose to remember how good it was to be together with my extended family for all those years (and all those years ago).

The Internet definition of "emotional resources" includes this: "Emotional resources are the most important resources because they keep people from returning to old habits. A lack of emotional resources refers to being able to choose and control emotional responses, particularly to negative situations, without engaging in self-destructive behavior." I think something was not quoted correctly, as it's the employment of emotional resources that keeps us from "engaging in self-destructive behavior" and not the lack of them. Or possibly it's saying, "Since there is a 'lack of emotional resources' you have to 'choose and control emotional responses.'" In either case, thinking about all of this has really helped me to deal with my feelings prompted by memories of past situations. This has also helped me to deal with the current news cycle as I am deeply disturbed by so much that I read and see. I have to choose not to deplete my emotional resources on things that I can't control (which is nearly everything).

The definition above also includes that "emotional resources are the most important resources." It doesn't state that they are some of the most important resources or are among the most important resources, it states that, "emotional resources are the most important resources." That includes a lot of resources! That suggests that emotional resources are more important than, for example, financial resources and relationship resources. And if you think about it, you will understand why. It's not what we have or whom we hang out with that makes us feel good or bad, but it's how we think about and respond to other resources that makes us feel good or bad.

I have recently been introduced to a Christian singer named Audrey Assad. Her song, "Drawn to You," has come to mean much to me. Drawn to you doesn't have to be God or Jesus or anything of a spiritual nature, it can be anything or anyone where you find hope, love, and joy instead of grief, pain, and sadness. Independence Day is as good a day as any to begin taking ownership of your emotions. It's not what has happened to us that affects the way we feel, but how we choose to remember these things and how we think about them. I challenge you to discover your emotional resources and to use them to find joy and fulfillment.

Ordinary Wonder

Transcendent: beyond or above the range of normal or merely physical human experience; surpassing the ordinary; existing apart from and not subject to the limitations of the material universe

Synonyms: supernatural, otherworldly, mystical, spiritual, sublime, ethereal

Antonyms: ordinary, mundane

I have had my share of encounters with the "transcendent." None of these happenings were drug or alcohol induced. I was not on anything. It's just that several different times in my life, something has broken through the fabric of the ordinary, the mundane, into some other dimension. What happened can only be described as "mystical" or "transcendent." These experiences left me dazed and somewhat bewildered. The upside of these experiences has been to put me in touch with a dimension of life that's beyond the ordinary. The downside of these experiences is that the ordinary in comparison feels mundane. If you remove the "extra" from "extraordinary" then the "ordinary" feels rather empty.

One of my transcendent experiences happened while driving on Highway 78 east from Jasper to Birmingham, Alabama. It involved beautiful music on the radio and a church I was passing along the way. There was no danger to me or other motorists as the whole incident only lasted a matter of seconds. But transcendence seems to happen out of time. The most powerful transcendent experience of my life came in a dream in 1982. When I woke up from the dream, I knew that my dream self was a part of a transformational experience. My dream self then transformed my waking self into something new. Thinking about the dream even now, thirty-seven years later, I am touched with its beauty, its power, and its purpose. Another transcendent experience was on a sailboat in the late 1980s. This experience temporarily filled me to overflowing with a sensation of buoyancy and wonder. Although I was very much in the body through the entire experience, my psyche seemed to float to somewhere else. From a passing of time perspective, this experience lasted about 20 minutes. This was considerably longer in duration than all of my other transcendental experiences combined. Another thing that separates this experience with the others is that something very similar happened at about the same time to my best friend, so for the first time I was able to talk to someone who understood what I was saying. Unfortunately, my friend got killed before we could talk about it again. Other mystical experiences have touched me and changed me over the years.

With this said, the secret to abundant living is not to rack up as many transcendent experiences as possible, but to find the extraordinary in the ordinary. This phenomenon is perhaps best illustrated in Thornton Wilder's play *Our Town*, when the events of one ordinary day in one ordinary town are transformed to the extraordinary. But we do not need to watch a play or sit under a Bodhi tree to see the extraordinary at work. Extraordinary things happen all around us every single day. The sun, which is 93 million miles away, has a surface temperature of about 6,000 degrees Fahrenheit. Yet after the heat and light have traveled their eight minutes to earth and have punctured Earth's atmosphere, the average temperature at the equator is only 88 degrees. With a little sunscreen, the heat of the sun is quite bearable to humans. Green living things on Earth use the light of the sun in a process called photosynthesis. This process synthesizes foods from carbon dioxide and water. Of all things, oxygen is a byproduct of this chemical interaction. Ninety-nine percent of the gases in our atmosphere are oxygen and nitrogen. A human being dies if deprived of oxygen for about five minutes. In the time you've spent reading this, your life has been spared because of your breathing. Amazing. That the Earth synthesizes enough oxygen every day for all seven billion of Earth's inhabitants is quite extraordinary.

UNICEF estimates that about 350,000 babies are born every day. That's 14,500 babies born every hour. Or, that's 243 living, breathing human beings born in the world every single minute of every day.

After nine months suspended in amniotic fluid, these tiny earthlings are now surviving on their own, breathing oxygen from the air like all of us. Isn't that extraordinary?! The world could not contain the books about the extraordinary things that happen to us every second of every day.

It has been quite some time since I have had a bona fide transcendental experience. Do I miss them? Of course I do. Do I need them? I must not or I would have them. The thing I miss the most about mystical experiences is the sense of existential arrival and departure that they provide. It's as though the experiences provide a cosmic signpost that reads, "You are here." So without some otherworldly guide to point the way, the Universe leaves that up to me. So what do I want to do with my life? Where do I go from here? I think I'll go to the kitchen and brew a cup of coffee. My Keurig is quite extraordinary.

Connections

"As you prepare to travel out in the world, remember it will always feel smaller with a little kindness. Because we know the most important connections we make aren't between places, they're between people." (Delta Airlines welcome video)

I've only been out of the country twice. During the summer of 1975, I traveled internationally on a college choir trip. Our main destination was a performance in Stockholm, but we also traveled and sang in Zurich, Oslo, Copenhagen, and London. Visiting that many countries in thirteen days was quite an undertaking. The musical highlight for me was singing in an ancient cathedral outside of Stockholm. Our choir had rehearsed and memorized German double motets in our practice room in Birmingham, Alabama. The two choirs divided on the risers and sang antiphonally. But then in that setting in Sweden, we divided across the chasm of the cathedral. In that split chancel choir loft, we sang those marvelous double motets where they were created to be sung. I sneaked a peak at the tourists below me who were transfixed by the beauty of the music as it echoed from wall to wall and ceiling to floor. I was transfixed as well. I'm affected as I think about it now.

Then in April of 2003, my wife and I spent a week in Santiago, Chile, with our son who was there on a college mission adventure. The highlight of that trip for me was a day trip to Viña del Mar. That place was the most beautiful ocean side setting I had ever visited. On a gloriously beautiful day, I witnessed the Pacific in all its majesty and splendor as the afternoon sun danced across the water and the breaking waves.

Delta suggests that the world is made smaller with kindness, and that is so true. But I would say that jets have a lot to do with that, too. I'm about a 90-mile drive to Atlanta and then about a 20-hour flight to nearly anywhere in the world. Delta's ready when I am, but I'm just not ready. You might say that I'm a domestic kind of a guy. Most of my life revolves around northwest Georgia and the greater Chattanooga area. I drive to Alabama and Indiana quite often to visit family and friends. I travel less often to Florida, Texas, Missouri, and Arkansas. And again, these places aren't about places, but about people. About twice a year, we let Delta take us to California to visit our son, daughter-in-law, and her family. Yes, in spite of local opinions to the contrary, California is part of the United States and is a domestic flight from Atlanta. So there you have it. Except for occasional vacation destinations, Georgia, Tennessee, Florida, California, Alabama, Indiana, Texas, Missouri, and Arkansas are pretty much where I "travel out in the world." The fjords of Norway without a doubt displayed the most incredible beauty I've ever witnessed. But every afternoon the sun sets over Lookout Mountain and I only need to walk out my front door to see it. The marvelous Cloudland Canyon is about a 30-minute drive from where I sit. The hiking trails and cascading waterfalls draw hundreds of thousands of hikers and spectators from all over the country to this state park every year. Fall Creek Falls State Park is about an hour northwest of here. It's as beautiful as it sounds.

Delta is right that the connections between people are more important than the connections between places, but for me to see those people Delta's connections are very important. When I step off the plane from Chattanooga into the terminal in Atlanta, I want to look at the digital board and see a flight, a gate, and a time of departure. And I hope and pray it all matches what's on my itinerary.

Delta Airlines ends its welcome video with, "Thank you for letting us be a part of your journey." My journey. That always catches me a bit off guard. I just think of it as a flight and Delta thinks of it as a journey. I think the next time my wife walks to the mailbox and back I'm going to ask, "How was your journey?" And she'll look at me and say, "Looks like we got some bills. Airmail."

Kyrie Eleison

[KEY ree eh ay LAY ee sohn]

The years 1973-1979 were crucible years. For three of those years I was in the Samford University A Cappella Choir. This experience provided the foundation for all the music I would create in the ensuing years. When our director, Dr. Black, gave the downbeat to start every rehearsal and performance, I was transported to an alternate reality; I became someone else. I was no longer David Helms from Enterprise struggling to catch up with the serious musicians on campus; I became part of the dynamic and living flow of music from medieval times to the present. I was as good as anybody else in the room. Much of who I am musically is because of that choir.

Most of these experiences at Samford came under the skillful direction of Dr. Black, but he did not conduct some of my most memorable music experiences. From time to time, our school of music hosted visiting conductors from all over the world. In this case, the conductor for this Catholic mass was a conductor from France. He didn't speak English and most of us didn't speak French. It became an interesting experiment in music and communication. He gave the downbeat for the powerful beginning and we sang "Kyrie" in a powerful descending octave. He said as he demonstrated with his arms, "NO, NO, NO! it's 'kEEereaa.'" So we sang it again and he said again, "NOOO. It's 'kEEEErEEaaa.'" This went on for nearly 30 minutes. At some point in the process, I got it. "Kyrie" took on a life of its own. I don't know if we ever sang it to his satisfaction or if he just gave up, but we moved on through the music. The performance as I remember was spectacular.

Although "Kyrie eleison" is translated, "Lord, have mercy," to this day when I pray for mercy, I don't pray, "Lord, have mercy on me," I pray,

"Kyrie eleison, Christe eleison." For me these words from the mass hold more power and authority than the English translation. Almighty God, I'm sure, understands the English, but the Latin, for me, expresses my feelings more deeply. And it feels like I'm speaking God's love language. Kyrie eleison is of Greek origin. The Greek gives the words their meaning; the Latin gives the words their power. Try it out for yourself. Roll Kyrie eleison around on your tongue and see how it feels. Whenever you're discouraged, "Kyrie eleison." When you think you've failed someone you love, "Kyrie eleison." When you think you've failed God, "Kyrie eleison." When you're hurting inside for any reason, "Kyrie eleison." When you feel like singing, "Kyrie eleison." "Kyrie," by Mr. Mister, actually rose to the top of the pop/rock charts in 1980. "Kyrie eleison down the road that I must travel. Kyrie eleison through the darkness of the night."

It took many years for me to figure out that people in other countries didn't have to mentally translate words into English before they understood them. Their words in their language defined the things and the thoughts in question. In Spain, they call the little green creatures that hop around on lily pads, "rana." In Paris, they live in a "maison." Not only do their words have meaning to them, but often there is no translation for certain words. Such is now the case for me with "Kyrie eleison and Christe eleison." I don't have to translate these powerful words; they speak for themselves.

I don't know what that French conductor learned from us, but I learned that if music is not raw power and raw emotion then why bother? "Kyrie eleison down the road that I must travel." I also learned the literal meaning of "the language of music." Music is its own country. Music is its own language. Words speak to the heart. Music touches the soul. "Kyrie eleison in the darkness of the night." I just didn't know how dark that night could be. But, "Blessed is the night; it reveals to us the stars." Unknown.

4'33"

I became fascinated with the music of John Cage (1912-1992) over 30 years ago. His philosophy was, in a nutshell, if it makes a sound, it's music. And by that he meant, "If it makes a sound, it's music." He believed that any noise or combination of noises was a legitimate musical expression. Anything. My favorite composition is his *Indeterminacy*, which is actually a combination of two compositions. He created a composition using a tape loop and hundreds of other sounds. Back in the reel-to-reel days you simply recorded something on tape, you cut the tape, taped it in a loop and recorded that loop over and over. Behind that constant loop he recorded a myriad of things. That was the first composition. The second composition involved Cage recording 90 seemingly unrelated stories with the first composition playing in the background. With the shorter stories, he talked rather slowly. With the longer stories, he talked very fast. I find the totality of the 90-minute composition to be quite profound.

But his most famous and most controversial composition is, by far, his *4'33"*. He originally composed this composition for piano, but it is now performed with full orchestra. The piano version involves the concert pianist walking to the piano, sitting down on the bench, opening the keyboard cover, and sitting absolutely still for four minutes and thirty-three seconds. The performer then closes the cover, stands and bows, and walks off the stage. In the full orchestral version, the conductor usually performs the work in three movements. There are two, two-minute movements and one movement of 33 seconds. With this version, the conductor takes the podium, raises his baton, but instead of giving a downbeat for the music to begin, he folds his hands in front of him. He remains motionless for two minutes. He then drops his hands. The audience and the performers are then free to relax and move, as they need to. The conductor then raises his baton and folds his hands for two more minutes. Again a break. He repeats this process for 33 seconds during the third and final movement. When the *4'33"* piece is complete, the conductor drops his arms, turns and bows, usually to thunderous applause.

The classical music world has a love/hate relationship with John Cage and with *4'33"* in particular. Many people feel that this "composition" is at best worthless and at worst an insult to serious music. How much skill does it require? How can you waste time on a program of serious music for this empty space? Other musicians and music goers consider this work to be a masterpiece of musical genius. After viewing the orchestral version several times on YouTube, I realized that it is very difficult for the performers and the audience to remain absolutely still and quiet. Noises happen. People cough, shuffle, and make a variety of noises. This gets recorded and becomes the performance. Then no performance of *4'33"* is exactly alike. This takes us back to Cage's basic philosophy of music, "If it makes a sound, it's music!" The orchestra and the audience are performing *4'33"*.

There is something else I noticed as I was viewing this performance of *4'33"*. While I was listening to it for the third time, I was thinking about what the piece meant. That led to another thought, "What does anything mean?" Who assigns meaning anyway? Classical music is accepted worldwide as "great music," but it is absolutely meaningless to millions of people. Some people would rather listen to a baby scream than listen to Bach, Beethoven, or Mozart. Who's to say? People assign their own meaning or lack thereof. Each of us assigns our own meaning to everything we see and do. Nothing is meaningful or aesthetically pleasing in and of itself. Some people listen to ear-splitting thump, thump in the car and other people never turn on the radio. In another context, I don't enjoy working in the yard but a neighbor down the street lives in her yard from daylight to dark. To each his own.

So *4'33"* is a level playing field for all of us. During the time, we think about anything we choose to think about, we let it mean anything we want it to mean. The only thing we share in common are the billions of neurons firing in our brains. With *4'33"*, we each create our own symphony in our heads. Make the performance as beautiful as you care to. Your version will not annoy anyone sitting on either side of you. I think it's very possible that some composer in the audience was inspired to compose some "great" work of art to be enjoyed by millions of concert goers and listeners. Now it's real(er).

I read a critique of this work a while back in the Wall Street Journal. I emailed the writer and asked him what would happen if you played *4'33"* backwards. He actually replied and said, "I've often wondered that myself, but was afraid to find out." Good sport! Oh, and why exactly *4'33"*? I imagine that John Cage felt that 4'34" would have been much too long. I know that it would be for me!

Acknowledgements

In the fall of 1971, I was a freshman at Enterprise State Junior College in Enterprise, Alabama. In freshman composition, Mr. Smith told me that I could write. I've been writing for the pure pleasure of writing ever since.

This book would never have come to be without the encouragement of my good friend Lynelle Mason. She has had several books published and encouraged me to do the same. I want to thank my cousin, Nancy Helms, who, after reading my blog, said, "David, you have become one of my favorite authors." I could never get "author" out of my head. This acknowledgement would not be complete without thanking the composers Mark McKenzie and Z. Randall Stroope. Quite often I was listening to their beautiful music while I was writing. I want to thank John Pierce and Lex Horton, who are both editors with Nurturing Faith. When I got off course, they both steered me in the right direction. I owe both of them a debt of gratitude.

I want to thank my blog readers who have already read most of this and encouraged me every step of the way. My friend, Peggy Posey, often told me, "Just keep writing!"

I want to thank my wife, Carolyn, for her time and dedication to this body of essays. Besides the many helpful corrections and suggestions, she typed and retyped every word on every page. I can't thank her enough. Finally, thank you to all of my family and friends who have encouraged me over the years to find my voice with words on a page. They encouraged me to be myself, tell my stories, and to write from my heart. This book is theirs just as much as it is mine.

www.ingramcontent.com/pod-product-compliance
Lightning Source LLC
Chambersburg PA
CBHW071008160426
43193CB00012B/1970